Robert Poynton

Do Conversation

There is no such thing as small talk.

BooK Co

To my sisters, Amanda and Lucy — for a lifetime of conversation.

Published by
The Do Book Company 2024
Works in Progress Publishing Ltd
thedobook.co

Text © Robert Poynton 2024
Photography © Jim Marsden 2024
Illustration © Nick Parker 2024

To find out more about our company,
books and authors, please visit
thedobook.co or follow us **@dobookco**

5 per cent of our proceeds from the sale
of this book is given to The DO Lectures
to help it achieve its aim of making
positive change: **thedolectures.com**

Cover designed by James Victore
Book designed and set by Ratiotype
Printed and bound by OZGraf Print on
Munken, an FSC® certified paper

MIX
Paper from
responsible sources
FSC® C163799

A CIP catalogue record for this book is
available from the British Library

ISBN 978-1-914168-27-7

10 9 8 7 6 5 4 3 2 1

Contents

1
That's what
I'm talking about

Conversation is remarkable. Somehow, by blurting out a stream of sounds, pulling a few faces and waving our hands around a bit, we are able to make meaning together. In a conversation, something appears amongst us that was not there before. There is a vast range of meanings we might make, everything from sweet nothings to bitter truths, but we do it all the time, everywhere — casually and formally, from the bus stop to the boardroom.

There is so much going on in conversation, on so many levels — physical, sensory, psychological, emotional, even metaphysical. It is so complex that it is amazing it works at all, and yet it does, in myriad ways. Exchanging information is only part of it. Conversation generates kaleidoscopic patterns that serve many purposes: we use it to think (and feel) together; develop relationships; play around; discover and learn; challenge authority; test and flesh out ideas; build worlds and forge identities. It goes to the heart of who we are. Conversation allows us to bridge the unfathomable gap between one experience of being human and another. It helps us cope with what philosopher John Gray calls 'the abiding disquiet that goes with being human'.

No wonder conversation is a source of both joy and anxiety. A lot rides on it. How I converse is part of what makes me, me. It shapes how others see me. Feeling loved and doing well may hinge upon it. Whatever you think or feel about conversation, whichever language you speak, whether you say a lot or a little, how you converse is part of who you are. In one sense, you are your conversation.

At home and at work we are entangled in elaborate webs woven with threads of conversation. More and more of our jobs are conversational not physical. Even if you dig ditches, you still talk about where and how to dig. And whilst you are digging, you can pass the time in conversation. Modern technology allows people to work at a distance from each other but only because it connects them virtually, creating new forms of conversation. The need may be met in different ways, but it doesn't go away. No one is an island.

The knack

Yet even though it is so common, we can feel anxiety about conversation. People often talk as if there is a knack to it that they somehow missed out on, as if there were a gene they lack but everyone else has, or were sick on the day it was taught at school.[1] There is a nagging feeling that if only you could just find the key, you would gain access to a land of ease and grace, where you are never stuck for words and you always come across as intelligent, accomplished and witty.

But it isn't genetic and there wasn't a class you missed. There is no secret sauce, no universal list of perfect

---

1   See the beautiful poem *'What you missed that day you were absent from fourth grade'* by Brad Aaron Modlin.

conversation starters, no keys to a kingdom of effortless conversational brilliance — not for you, or anyone else. The illusion that there is can lead you to squander time and energy in a futile pursuit. Or it might depress you so much that you give up before you start — deciding you just don't have what it takes, so there is no point in trying.

Yet you are amazing at conversation already. We all are. I want to celebrate that. To be able to converse at all, at whatever level, is an extraordinarily complex and sophisticated skill we take almost entirely for granted. The intricate dance of words and gestures we routinely engage in is a delightful human capacity, hiding in plain sight.

No other beings or intelligence (whether animal or artificial) can converse the way we do. We often fail to appreciate how difficult the 'easy' things are and how remarkable it is that we learn them at all. Acknowledging this is important. To get more from conversation, you first need to accept how astonishingly complex it is.

This is no excuse for complacency. As the Zen master Shunryu Suzuki said to his students: 'Each of you is perfect the way you are: and you can use a little improvement.' Something similar applies here. You might baulk at this and be convinced of your own ability (or lack of it) but your capacity for conversation isn't fixed. You don't either possess it or not, like brown eyes or black hair. There are times when you feel awkward and others when you light up. In conversation, disaster and triumph are both impostors. This is true for everyone. We are all works in progress, immersed in and sensitive to a context that has many layers, able to wield a wide array of skills and stratagems, consciously and unconsciously, to navigate our way across the messy yet magical terrain of conversation. That's what I'm talking about.

It's not what it used to be

Conversation appears to be under siege — from technology, globalism and the pace of modern life in general. It is often said that conversation is not what it used to be: but then it never was. Thinkers and writers throughout history, including Nietzsche, Montaigne and Cicero, all expressed concern about the decline of conversation.

How we talk together, what we talk about, what we make of (and with) our conversation is always shifting. However, that doesn't necessarily mean it is a capacity we are about to lose. In fact, conversation itself is the cause of much of the change that we (and it) are subject to. It is the ceaseless, bubbling brew of conversations in fields, homes, offices, bars, coffee shops, workshops, laboratories and garages all over the world that gives birth to new ideas, discoveries, technologies, movements, protests or identities. These, in turn, change conversation itself.

Human society is a vast constellation of intricate conversational niches, with contrasting, competing, conflicting and complementary conversations in all kinds of languages, in a gloriously complex and entangled babble. But we don't normally think of conversation this way (if we think about it at all).

Psychologist Adam Mastroianni studies 'how people perceive and misperceive their social worlds'. Much of his work focuses on what happens when people talk face-to-face. The images he uses to describe conversation have been helpful and illuminating for me. He says: 'Talking to another person is like rock climbing, except you are my rock wall and I am yours. If you reach up, I can grab on to your hand, and we can both hoist ourselves skyward. Maybe that's why a really good conversation feels a little bit like floating.'

I love this idea — that through conversation we can help each other up, to a place we could never reach alone, where we don't even touch the ground.

Who am I to talk about conversation?

My interest is not in the scientific analysis of conversation, nor is it in the idea of conversation as an art, dying or otherwise. I am curious about this ordinary–extraordinary thing we do every day: what makes it possible and what does it, in turn, make possible? It is more than a social skill or a medium of communication. I want to explore (and marvel at) its complexity, subtlety and richness, and I hope you will join me on that exploration. I want to invite you to wonder, in both senses of the word: to be curious in the way that leads to practical learning, but also to become fascinated, even in awe, of what we can do in conversation. As a result, you will understand more about how it works and thus be able to do yet more with it, more consciously.

This interest prompted an inquiry into my own experience of conversation and that of the people I talk with — so what is that experience? Conversation not only feeds my work, it *is* my work. I design and facilitate workshops, programmes and events for businesses, organisations or individuals that are, in large measure, conversations. It is also through conversation that I develop the ideas and build the relationships that feed into them. So I spend a lot of time in what would be regarded by many people as 'idle' conversation.[2]

---

2   One friend of mine says that I have made a career out of 'mucking about'. He's not wrong, but there is a lot you can learn that way.

For example, a few weeks back my day began (on Zoom) talking with a former BBC journalist who teaches creative writing at the University of Central Asia in Kyrgyzstan. We explored the challenges and the creative possibilities of working across different languages and cultures. A little later I went outside and bumped into my neighbour Vicente, who farms the land around our house in rural Spain. Some stones had fallen from the wall that separates our track from his olive grove so we started talking about boundaries — a sensitive topic at the moment as the land registry is being digitised.

'The bureaucrats can draw whatever lines they like on their maps, but the wall is where it is and you and I both know that,' he said, smiling mischievously. He may have spent his whole life farming but his observations and insights got me thinking about the difference between the legal, social and physical boundaries and the dangers of abstraction.

Later on that day, I spoke with Colonel Jason 'TOGA' Trew, Dean and Commandant of the US Air Force strategy school in Montgomery, Alabama. Jason contacted me about a year ago after I appeared on a podcast about the value of play and we have been talking regularly ever since. Even though he is a military man, none of our conversations have a specific objective and yet they are anything but 'idle'. Ideas, insights and energy emerge from seemingly trivial observations about flying suits, scaffolding or Lego. We laugh a lot and learn things we never could alone.

This isn't unusual. As well as military officers like Jason, the A to Z of my conversational partners includes academics, actors, artists, breath and body workers, CEOs, civil servants, designers, diplomats, doctors, filmmakers, musicians, philosophers, photographers, writers and a Zen priest. The conversational soup I live and work in has many ingredients.

These individual conversations feed the conversations I host and hold with groups. As long ago as 1998, I ran an event that brought people from all over the world for a long weekend in Spain that became known as 'The Conversation'. Twenty five years later, following the pandemic, I created a contemporary expression of that same enthusiasm. 'Yellow' convened small groups of people online, offering a space for them to reflect through regular conversations that unfolded over the course of months. My partner Alex Carabi and I have designed and held over two hundred of these conversations, which, as one participant put it 'expand and shift my understanding in ways I can't anticipate but sorely need'.

Yellow itself was born out of my experience at the Saïd Business School, at the University of Oxford. There, I have worked on the Strategic Leadership Programme (one of their executive education programmes) for over twenty years — a course designed as a week-long vessel for conversation.

Even the workshops I do using improvisational theatre, which involve physical exercises and games, hinge on conversation. They are not about comedy, they are about developing the ability to navigate complexity and uncertainty and it is in the reflective conversations that the learning lies.

About this book

This book is the result of my own curiosity and the inquiry it gave birth to. Your own experience and your interests will be different from mine, but you already know a lot, even if it doesn't feel that way. Acknowledging that we are already good at something difficult encourages us to develop the skill further. By contrast, beating ourselves up about it, individually or collectively, is not very helpful.

For me, conversation isn't a problem to be solved but an experience to be lived. Thus you won't find me recommending a 'right' way to converse, or offering a step-by-step method. It would be perverse if I did, because reducing conversation to a formula is a sure way to destroy it. Instead of trying to pin conversation down, it is far more fitting, fruitful and fun to play around with it.

I encourage you to do the same. Start your own inquiry. Mess with my ideas, take what works for you, ignore what doesn't and add your own. What is on offer here is more about a way of being in the world than acquiring a technique which will make you look good. Conversation is, after all, something we do together.

When exploring, having a guide can help. Though I don't know where you might be hoping to get to, having spent a lot of time wandering around the terrain of conversation I have a feel for the landscape and what to watch out for along the way.

There are stories, tools, new language, models and frameworks (plural) and, at the end, even a numbered list of 'maxims and mantras', but none of them are definitive or complete. As with any kind of learning worth engaging in, you need to bring something of yourself to it.

To help you plot your own way around the material, let me signpost what you will find where.

Chapter 2 — An everyday miracle

This explains why I see conversation as 'an everyday miracle' and explores the idea that conversation generates a 'field' of its own.

Chapter 3 — What to do in conversation

The focus here is on what you can do *as an individual* to participate in creating fruitful conversation. A theme is that conversation is as much about the body as it is about the mind.

Chapter 4 — Improvised conversation

Conversation is always responsive, so it cannot be scripted, you have to improvise. I apply my own simple model (from *Do Improvise*) to conversation specifically and offer additional improv tools, models and language that also map neatly onto conversation.

Chapter 5 — To host and to hold

You can create the conditions for more satisfying conversations, whether you have a formal convening role or not. There are four fundamental questions to consider and a raft of ideas that increase the chances of having a good conversation before you even start to talk.

Chapter 6 — Everything changes, everything stays the same

Our response to the way technology changes our conversation is creative and vibrant, though we often don't recognise it. We invent novel formats and new ways of conversing and we also return to old practices, showing what doesn't change.

Chapter 7 — Maxims and mantras

To summarise and synthesise what I have learned I compiled my own numbered list, but what I am really doing is encouraging you to make your own.

Though I didn't plan it that way, it turns out that these ideas are intimately related to both improvisation and pause (both of which I have written about before) and the books flow into and out of each other, exploring related questions from different angles.

Many people told me that they read *Do Pause* slowly, which was fitting. Perhaps something equally appropriate will happen with this one? It is the product of hundreds, if not thousands, of conversations: I hope it will be the source of many more.

2
An everyday miracle

Conversation is bafflingly complex. There are so many different layers to it. To start with, we have to be able to hear a stream of sounds as meaningful words, something technology still struggles with. The voice recognition software I use frequently hears 'Business School' as 'business cool'. You wouldn't make that mistake: people turn sound into living units of meaning immediately and effortlessly.

Occasionally, some of the complexity we routinely deal with in conversation becomes visible. Many years ago, as I stood in a queue in a bank in rural China, an old man approached me, ranting and shouting, grabbing at me and waving his arms. At least, that was what I experienced. It turned out he was trying to help me, by pointing out that the bank for foreigners was across the road. Ignorant of Chinese and deaf to its tonal inflections, all I heard was a barrage of noise.

When I was learning Spanish I remember the magical moment when words started to appear out of a stream of meaningless sound, like road signs emerging from thick fog. And yet as soon as I passed that point I forgot there ever was any fog. With our native tongue we hear a flow of meaningful words that have *always* had shape and colour and we can't stop hearing this way any more than we can see a scrolling display as a series of stationary blinking lights.

Hearing sound as distinct and meaningful words is hard enough, but it is only the beginning of the complexity we have to navigate in conversation. The number of cues and clues we pick up is immense and the precision with which we do so is extraordinary. Whether we realise it or not, we are sensitive to the *feel* of the words we hear, as well as their meaning — to the tone in which they are said: the volume, pitch, rhythm, cadence and inflection. We make sense of what isn't there — the pauses and the silence. We begin to learn the music of the human voice when we are still in our mother's womb. We read physical cues such as the angle, position and movement of the head, hands and body, including tiny dynamic details of posture, gesture and eye movement. We pick these up even if we can't see the other person — you can sense someone's physicality, even on the phone. Conversation is intimate, personal and only possible at a small scale.

Conversation is also always contextual. 'Silly man' could be a reproach or a term of endearment, depending upon the circumstances. We weigh up a host of contextual questions without conscious thought. Questions like: Who are you talking to? What for? What hopes, intentions and expectations are in play? Are you at home or at work? Are you next to the person you are talking to, in front of them, across the room from them or online? Are you standing, sitting, lying? We take all of this (and more) into account and make constant adjustments to our behaviour, many of them microscopic. Much of conversation happens below the threshold of consciousness.

You are also able to shift between different registers of slang or jargon that exist within a family, organisation or subculture. You factor in the history, temperament, character and interests of the people you are talking to (and your relationship with them) along with the cultural differences of country, region, profession or tribe you are each part of.

Almost nothing, then: yet we make light of it.

This doesn't mean we necessarily get it 'right'. There is still plenty of room for misunderstanding. Nonetheless, we make sense of what is said — even if the sense we make isn't always quite what the person speaking had in mind.

One natural response to all this complexity is to try and reduce it to something simpler. Lists like 'seven ways to speak up at work' or 'five questions to break an awkward silence' make it *too* simple, offering advice like 'always start a conversation with a question that has a definite numerical answer'. However, whilst there may be occasions when that will help, if you aren't able to judge when that moment is, it is as likely to kill the conversation as nourish it. You can't make it a rule.

Expecting a checklist to produce good conversation is like expecting painting by numbers to produce a work of art. If I am in conversation with you, I can't be following a list, I need to be paying attention to you and me, here and now. Conversation doesn't work by rote. It is a living, breathing flow, not a collection of shiny objects.

The illusion of control

One of the reasons we are drawn to social media is because it reduces the complexity of live interaction and offers the promise of control. You can correct or polish what you put out, testing different versions to see which 'work' best (assuming that getting more 'likes' is a sign of it 'working').

However, this is also a shortcoming. Projecting a simplified, often idealised version of yourself can distance you from others. Social media connects you to your phone more than it connects you to other people and encourages you to talk about what is on that phone not what's on your mind. So in many ways, social media isn't very sociable. When you 'friend' or 'follow' someone, you just tether yourself to them, whereas in live conversation you become entangled with each other. The 'rough magic' of that entanglement is lost when everything becomes too polished.

In all the furore about technology we often forget how recent this all is and that we have little idea how it will work out. Moreover, 'digital natives' (like my children) understand and use technology quite differently from 'digital immigrants' (like me) and as a result have a different view of what constitutes conversation. But whether you delight in it or damn it (and it tends to be one of the two) social media is undoubtedly different from live conversation. One isn't a substitute for the other, each has qualities the other lacks. It isn't a sharp divide — conversation only happening face to face and something else entirely happening via technology. And whilst it undoubtedly changes things, it is a leap to suppose that social media will wipe what we have been doing for millennia completely off the map.

However, it is significant that social media is shaped by a worldview based on 'optimisation'. For people in the tech world, the most natural thing in the world to do is to 'optimise' everything, including conversation. For example, in a podcast entitled 'The Art of Conversation' one techie argued, without irony, that the goal is simply to get what you want as quickly as possible then get out, reducing conversation to mere transaction. Anything else he saw as unnecessary decoration. For him the 'art' was to avoid conversation altogether.

What would an optimum conversation be, anyway? Do you always know what you mean or what you want? I certainly don't. I might say something to hear how it sounds, see what it sparks off in others or make visible what I don't understand. Someone else will often make sense of it for me. When my conversational partners go off at tangents or interpret what I say in a way I hadn't imagined I don't see this as failure: indeed, it is often exactly what I am looking for. I am less interested in trying to transmit or 'solve' something than in making meaning or weaving worlds together. Conversation is more a play of minds than a transfer of data.

There is a parallel with food. Elon Musk said that if he could pop a pill which gave him all the nourishment he needed, he would do so to save the time and energy 'wasted' on meals. This betrays an assumption that food is just fuel. It ignores the sensual, social and cultural nourishment of eating. Similarly, to see conversation as a mere transaction simplifies things, but at the cost of ignoring or eliminating much of what it does for us.

Blunders, inanities and foolishness

The branch of social science known as 'Conversational Analysis' does exactly what it says. It seeks to understand talk and conversation (which it regards as much the same thing) through data, measurement and analysis.

Researchers pay close attention to the fact that the words we speak are vessels freighted with emotional and relational baggage, which is where much of the action is. Conversation is not just about the messages but the 'meta-messages'.

From this perspective 'the relationship is the conversation', 'the problem is the process' and we often misunderstand each other because we have different conversational styles. There is a (communication) problem to be solved and the ideal conversation is one where we properly understand precisely what others mean.

The general conclusion is that we don't do it very well. It is striking that the study of conversation can lead to such a bleak view of it. Instead of recognising the extraordinary complexity involved, the focus is often on misunderstanding, miscommunication and failure, as if that is all there is. In her book *That's Not What I Meant!* (one of many titles which play on the negative) the conversational analyst Deborah Tannen says: 'Every social encounter is rich with blunders, inanities and foolishness. Very little of what is said is really apt. Still less important. Still less eloquent.'

That is not my experience. Many of my conversations, particularly those with local people in rural Spain, may be thick with 'blunders, inanities and foolishness' but I cherish them nonetheless. They enable us to show affection, be 'seen' by each other, take delight in the beauty of our surroundings and so on. Moreover, almost any conversation, however clumsy, can show me something I haven't thought of, spark off new ideas or bring me energy, even if I don't completely understand what the other person means — something which is always possible when you are speaking a second language in a rural backwater. There is more to conversation than eloquence and much to be said for fumbling around.

Fernando Flores, a Chilean philosopher and computer scientist, suggests that language is not just a tool for conveying information, but is also a way of creating and shaping our social reality. He identifies three different kinds of conversation, each with a different focus. They are: conversations for action; conversations for possibility; and conversations for understanding. In this way of looking you are either focused on trying to get stuff done, generating new ideas or building shared understanding.

When I am thinking about how to frame a conversation that I am convening (see Chapter 5) these categories come in handy. However, though it is a beguiling idea, conversation is rarely as neat and tidy as this. Whatever I intend, a conversation can veer from one type to another in a heartbeat. Even if I were able to constrain them to just one type, I am not sure I would want to. A single conversation might blend different kinds and be the richer for it. This is a feature not a bug. It is in the nature of conversation not to adhere to any particular script, plan or framing.

What is conversation for?

These attempts to reduce conversation to something simple enough to understand assume that it is *for* something. Yet one widely used definition is that conversation is precisely that kind of talk that is not *for* anything. It is an end in itself (in academic language it is 'autotelic'). By this measure, if there is something specific you want — to please your boss, get some information, or sell something — you may be talking but it wouldn't qualify as conversation.

Former FBI negotiator Chris Voss makes this distinction in a podcast with Lex Fridman. He says that in a negotiation: 'we are both aware of a problem we are trying to solve.' He contrasts that to the podcast conversation where: 'I rolled in here not having any expectations, to hear your questions and what interests you.' There is no problem to solve.

If conversation is not about solving problems, transmitting a message or getting a result you want, then another possibility is that it is simply a pleasure in itself. In the 18th century this idea was pervasive. Conversation was regarded as a social art and an essential part of civil society. People were lauded for their use of language, depth of knowledge and, perhaps above all, for their wit. A person's social and intellectual standing was judged by how they performed in conversation. Benjamin Franklin, Samuel Johnson and literary critic Elizabeth Montagu became 'celebrity' conversationalists. In this view, the heyday of conversation was the Paris salons or London coffee houses of the 17th and 18th centuries, and it has been in decline ever since.

This idea casts a long shadow. Even today, the feeling that in conversation we should appear to be knowledgeable, clever, accomplished or funny is widely assumed, even if it is rarely acknowledged. This is intimidating. It creates pressure to perform and feels like a kind of examination. The very idea that conversation *ought* to be a pleasure can be precisely what makes it forbidding.

A life of its own

For me, the hallmark of a good conversation is that something appears which was not there before. Conversation is 'a process of becoming, becoming'.[1] That is what brings it alive. We are not just passing sealed packages back and forth, or signalling to each other, we are weaving something together that takes on a life of its own.

---

1   This is borrowed from Kevin Kelly, editor at large of *Wired* magazine, who said, 'Life is a process of becoming, becoming.'

It is not within any of the individuals, it appears between them. Conversation is that space where different perspectives, ideas, observations and experiences meet, blend, mutate and spark off each other. It is more than the sum of what has been said. We emerge changed. A field is created that we are all in touch with, which connects and contains us, but which no one controls. This field can endure over time, with particular conversations both feeding off it and feeding into it. As historian Theodore Zeldin says, 'Conversation doesn't just shuffle the pack, it creates new cards.'

There is something paradoxical about this. Conversation is an end in itself and yet it serves many purposes. You get something by not aiming for anything. The tighter you grip on to what you want, the less likely you are to get it. It is the tension inherent in these paradoxes that means you never quite know what will happen, which is why conversation has the power to delight and amaze us.

The upside of this complexity and uncertainty is that you can always be surprised. What will appear in a conversation cannot be known in advance. A conversation I stumbled into recently shifted my mood, taught me new facts, sparked off ideas for this book, gave me a new perspective on the phenomenon of consciousness and revitalised a relationship. All of this came out of the blue, just as I was about to leave to catch a train.

The last of these effects is perhaps the most powerful of all. Somehow, in conversation I am able to catch a glimpse of other human beings, having their own unique experience of being human, just as I am. This means I am not alone. It creates an inescapable feeling that there are others like me, who are *not* me, that I can connect with through conversation. And because they are like me, but *not* me, as I become entangled with them, my understanding and experience of what it is to be human is expanded. I am tested and challenged; enlarged and enriched; stretched and reshaped. In conversation, we don't just talk with individuals, we encounter entire worlds, each with their own deep, complex histories.

This shouldn't be possible. By definition, the only experience I have is my own. I don't have any access to whether you are hungry, or thirsty, or thinking of Vienna.[2] I am locked into my own experience (as are you). All the sounds, images, memories and understandings I use to infer the existence not just of another human body, but of another human experience, are part of my own perception. The connection we are able to conjure up together is a kind of illusion and yet, to me, it feels as real as anything can be. This is incomprehensible and yet it happens all the time. Which is why I think of conversation as an everyday miracle. The miracle isn't that we can talk to people across the world using technology, amazing though that is, or that it is a wonderful way to build ideas, take decisions or share knowledge. It is both more and less than that — the miracle is that we can have any kind of meaningful conversation with another human being at all.

Mysteries like this are not so unusual. For example, a magnetic field is an 'invisible force' that has no substance, yet every electric motor in the world relies on one. Perhaps one day we might discover that the idea of a conversational field is more than just a metaphor?

Conversation is an everyday miracle we can all work. It is part of the fabric of our lives. Once you recognise how complex and paradoxical it is, you can accept both how amazing you are at it and how much more you could

---

2   I owe this phrase to Dr Kathy Wilkes, who used it in a discussion of the philosophical problem of 'other minds' in a revision class in 1985.

get from it. There is more to this than technique and it is not a process you can ever control. It is more like sailing a boat — where you have to take account of wind, tide and current — than driving a car. But that doesn't mean there is nothing you can do to improve your conversation. You need to be willing to engage with your whole person, to try and fail and try again, which is uncomfortable. But that is exactly what it means to practise.

Conversation is
an everyday miracle
we can all work.
It is part of the
fabric of our lives.

3
**What to do
in conversation**

In conversation you really only do two things. You speak and you listen. There are infinite combinations and variations but, in essence, that is all there is.

Yet people offering advice on conversation sometimes talk as if only one or the other matters. There is a minor industry devoted to 'killer questions' and 'conversation starters' as if the 'right' words will unlock everything and being a competent, capable person depends upon finding them.

But conversation doesn't just ride on what you say. If you want your children to talk to you, it is less about finding the 'right' question to ask than it is about showing them — day in, day out — that you are listening, interested and curious. Presence and patience count for more than clever questions. This also applies in other contexts, like work. As leadership coach Susan Scott says, a 'dazzling way with words' is not enough to 'guarantee success as a leader'.

The focus on what to say keeps you thinking about yourself, shrinking your field of attention to how you are 'performing'. Yet conversation is a collective endeavour, not an individual one. The question isn't 'how do you shine?' but 'how do you contribute?'

There is more to it than listening

There is another set of people, often journalists and researchers, who treat conversation as if it were just like an interview and focus almost exclusively on listening. Yet in a conversation getting someone else to talk is only half of it. Julie Batty worked on the BBC radio show *Desert Island Discs*. Her job was to meet the interviewees in advance of the show and get them to relax and open up. She was brilliant at it, mastering the 'soft eyes and ears' necessary to listen deeply.[1] As a result, sometimes the interviewee would want to meet up again. When they did it was invariably disappointing because the way Julie had paid attention to them was part of her professional role. When they met as individuals it needed to be reciprocal. Paying attention can't be just one way. It requires both give and take from everyone involved.

Listening can be generous, but so can speaking. Your words can spark off ideas or trains of thought, make sense of things or share a truth that others connect with. Speaking can be selfish, but so can listening. If you only listen, you take little responsibility or risk and give others little to work with.

Some approaches do recognise the value of both. In *The Fifth Discipline Fieldbook*, MIT professor Peter Senge wrote about the need to balance 'advocacy' and 'inquiry' to create what he called 'skilful conversation'. This frames conversation as a form of reasoning and the language has a legal feel to it, but the basic idea is a good one. On the one hand we need to be willing to offer things up for other people to respond to (advocacy) and on the other we need to invite them to contribute (inquiry). However, rather

---

1   The idea of 'soft eyes and ears' is from Susan Scott's book *Fierce Conversations*.

than 'balance' the two sides equally, I think it is more powerful to think about how you weave the two together.

Practise makes perfect

There are no rules

Rules are of limited use here. The rules of a game tell you about the constraints of the 'field' but they don't tell you how to play. Nothing works all the time. Instead, develop a practice. A practice is something you do and keep doing. It means trying things out for yourself and being prepared to fail, so you have to be patient, gentle and forgiving towards yourself. There is no end point, finish line or final score—just more practise. Writer and podcaster Sam Harris says: 'All of those moments that seem like a recognition of failure, are in fact, the practice.' He is talking about mindfulness, but the same is true of conversation. At any moment you are free to begin again.

Don't practise avoidance

The way to develop a practice of conversation is by having conversations. Who knew? The practice is the thing itself. The more you do it, the easier it gets. Obvious though that may be, you can easily slip into a pattern of avoidance. The 'digital natives' Sherry Turkle interviewed for her book *Reclaiming Conversation* recognised that they needed to have conversations to get good at them but constantly used their phones to put that moment off. But you don't get good at anything by avoiding it. Even in an age of digital media, conversation is everyday stuff, so the chance to practise is always at hand.

It is easy to miss this. A few weeks back, boarding a crowded tube train in London, I noticed a man with his bags on the seat next to him. I glowered at him and he gestured towards the bags, wordlessly asking me if I wanted him to move them. With another gesture, I declined. Our silent exchange over, I buried my nose in a book and the train pulled away.

At the next stop, an elderly man with a stick struggled to get on. 'I don't recommend getting old,' he announced to anyone willing to listen, laughing. The man with the bags smiled, cleared them off the seat and offered it to the elderly man, who sat down beaming. He immediately asked the 'bag man' where he was going and they happily fell into conversation about London, health and the BBC. The simple humanity of the exchange emanated warmth and the two of them were still chatting away when I got off. It was a stark contrast to the curt, distant, judgemental exchange I had instigated. The elderly man was wiser than me; rather than avoid the conversation, he embraced it.

Strangers on a train

Of course, most of us dread talking to strangers on a train. We expect it to be awkward and difficult. Which is why researchers ask people to do it. When they do, people who expect it to be a negative experience discover exactly the opposite. We are often wrong about what will be conducive to our happiness.

Think about this the next time you shy away from a conversation. How many opportunities are there that you don't take or even notice? Of course, there is a risk in talking to others. You don't know how it will play out, you have to be willing to be vulnerable and make a little effort, but that is what makes it worthwhile. Getting good at conversation is a bit like getting fit: 'no pain, no gain'. That day on the tube I wasn't willing to make the effort. The elderly man was and as a result he went on his way a little richer, having had a warm, human exchange — a gift he also gave to the bag man. Of such threads our lives are woven.

You don't have to start by talking to strangers on trains (though you could) but you do need to practise. To distance yourself from conversation is to distance yourself from the messy business of life itself. There is no way around it, you have to go through.

Talk to different people

If you have the chance to talk with farmers, florists or philosophers, so much the better. The greater the variety of people you converse with, the more your world expands. When people come to Oxford for a leadership programme what they value most is the chance to talk with 'friendly strangers'. In doing so, they discover both new perspectives and common struggles.

With the whole world online it is easier than ever to join a conversation with people who aren't like you. Talk to people of a different age or from a different place. Talk to gamers, gardeners or gun owners. To do so, you have to be willing to feel out of your depth, confused or ignorant. Which is an attitude you have to cultivate.

For example, after an event I organised in London we went to the pub (as you do). One of the participants was explaining how much he had enjoyed talking to people from other professions whilst studying for his MBA. Yet there he was, talking to the two colleagues he had come with, who, like him, were accountants. He missed the chance to strike up a conversation with the people he had already met in the workshop and who were standing at the bar — a group which included a novelist, an evolutionary biologist and several musicians.

The practice of speaking to different kinds of people breaks you out of your own (little) world. The point isn't to learn about writing, fruit flies or medieval madrigals, though you might. The point is what it does to you. By talking to academics in Oxford and farmers in rural Spain, I experience, first hand, that there are different ways of knowing things as well as different things to know. I am reminded that a conversation can serve very different purposes — to test ideas or anchor you in the landscape. Conversations like this make you aware of what you take for granted. You have the chance to see yourself and your own assumptions.

Open doors

There is an image I picked up from psychologist Adam Mastroianni, which is a fantastic device for thinking about how you contribute to conversations. This is the idea of a 'doorknob'. I love it partly because it is such a funny word, but also because it is so graphic and useful. A doorknob opens something. In conversation, 'doorknobs' are 'digressions and confessions and bold claims that beg for a rejoinder'. Something as simple as an unusual word or a vivid image can act as a doorknob. Whatever it is, it invites a response of many kinds — it is a 'set-up' that has many possible 'pay-offs'.

In a recent conversation with two friends, the word 'wallah' opened a door to a conversation about the racism of 1970s British comedy, Marxists in rural India, hockey, autism, family reconciliation, the RAF in France in 1940 and why my father played the piano. A single, unusual word sparked off a wealth of connections, ideas and stories we could not have anticipated. Obliques and tangents are only a distraction if you have a fixed destination, so don't automatically apologise for them or frown upon them — they often lead somewhere interesting.

'Confessions' is another part of Mastroianni's definition. This is the bit that requires a little bravery. What you 'confess' doesn't have to be intimate, but to work as a doorknob it does need to be somehow unexpected, novel or provocative. By putting something out yourself you give others something to respond to. You might confess a passion for train sets, synchronised swimming or flower arranging — a 'bit that doesn't fit' (to borrow a term from actors, who look for that to give a character depth). You might open up about how you are feeling right now. You might be self-deprecating and talk about a struggle or a failing, but whatever it is, it needs to be true for you and reveal something of yourself. A small act of bravery acts as a doorknob because it invites others to share their own truths too.

Another form of doorknob is incompleteness. My friend and Oxford colleague Tracey Camilleri describes herself as a 'half a sentence person'. Conversations with Tracey are littered with thoughts she begins but allows you to end. This makes working with her easy and effective. Her willingness to leave things unfinished invites other people to add their perspective.

Another incident with a stranger on a train illustrates how simple this can be. Boarding a crammed train, I found my seat was littered with empty wine bottles and sandwich packets left by the previous passenger. As I struggled to clear them away, the young woman in the next seat offered to help by taking the book I was holding (*Hello World* by

Hannah Fry). When I sat down she gave it back and asked: 'Is it any good?' An hour or so later, we were deep in conversation about whether she should take a year off after university or try to get a job straight away. At the time, *Do Pause* had just been published and I had some copies with me, so just before I got off, I gave her one.

Get curious about what kind of doorknobs might work for you. Books work for me, though it took me a while to work that out. I assumed that when people came from far afield to spend a weekend in Spain reading, the books themselves were important, but it turned out that they were just points of departure for long, branching conversations that go on for hours over meals and late into the night, often spanning the whole weekend. For you it could be music, food, movies, sport or poetry. Whatever it is, once you have the idea of 'doorknobs' you will start to spot them and use them in conversation.

Don't be too sure of yourself

Being certain is something we aspire to. Making ourselves vulnerable, on the other hand, raises the fear of being seen as weak. But in conversation, if you are too sure of yourself it leaves little room for anyone else.

This shows up as tightly held points of view, delivered in an uncompromising way. In Spanish these are called *banderitas*—little flags we plant in conversation as if claiming territory or making conquest, which don't make space for other views. For example, 'We locals don't need outsiders interfering'. Similarly, being a 'smug explainer' doesn't help open up conversation.

There are clues in the language to look out for. It is easy to slip from the indefinite to the definite article so that 'a problem' becomes '*the* problem' (or '*the* question' or '*the* truth'). Phrases like 'in reality' or 'the point is' become routine. Crisp numbered lists add certainty and high-status plays are common (take it from me, I am the author here).

To sum up (another technique used to corral the conversation):

1. Statements are definitive
2. The tone is clipped and curt
3. Gestures are sharp and pointed
4. Questions are closed

Have you got that?

If so, you might want to let go of it. It can bludgeon others into passivity, leaving you with what novelist Chimamanda Ngozi Adichie calls the 'single story'. Or it might create unnecessary and corrosive conflict. Relax your grip on certainty and make 'not knowing' part of your practice. Allow yourself to be confused and to acknowledge that. Be prepared to contradict yourself — changing your mind is one way to expand it. Life is not a debating society. Conversation is not an argument you are trying to win.

People rarely make a conscious decision to dominate, but some kinds of people are allowed (even expected) to be dominant, whereas others aren't. Those most likely to dominate, for example middle-aged white men (like me), are often oblivious to this bias and there are times when it is important to point that out. However, that isn't always the place to start. Whoever you are, look at your own patterns as well.

One way to do this is to practise 'speaking from the I'. Saying 'you' or 'we' instead makes assumptions about how others think or feel. There is a big difference between:

'*you* know how, when *you* get upset *you*...' and: 'when *I* get upset what *I* find is...'

Speak for yourself, not others. Present your own experience as exactly that, don't turn it into a general truth.

Mucking about also helps. Seriously. Levity does more than add light relief, welcome though that may be. Playfulness and humour release energy and shift the mood. They invite novelty and make assumptions visible. Humour allows you to explore 'what ifs' without premature judgement. Using irreverence breaks boundaries and lets more into the conversation, which is quite different from trying to show how witty you are.

Humour also makes conversations memorable. It is more than 15 years since Marshall Young, then the dean of an Oxford college, described the university as a 'medieval theme park' but it still tickles me, and it gets me thinking about the power of place (something we will get to in Chapter 5).

Pay attention

We live in a noisy, distracted world where attention is in short supply, so pay attention to how you pay attention. Make that part of your practice. This is wider and deeper than simply listening politely to others. As novelist George Saunders points out, 'One of the main symptoms of a bad conversation is this: one of the participants is on auto-pilot.' Attention is the unspoken ingredient of conversation. If you pay more attention to attention itself —to how you listen and what you notice—it takes the pressure off worrying about what to say. It shifts your focus, acting as a reminder that it isn't all about you.

Much has been written about different levels of listening—from 'downloading' to 'generative listening'.

However many levels of listening you identify and whatever you call them, the models confirm what you already know — that you can listen superficially or deeply. And if you pay attention to how you pay attention, you will know when you are doing which.

Hearing happens automatically but listening takes an effort. When you make that effort, you participate in a conversation just as much as when you speak. When you are listening deeply it shows up in your posture, position and stance, so you don't have to work mechanically at creating eye contact or smiling, that all happens naturally. When people feel heard, they slow down and say less, which creates time and space for thought.

Giving your attention — to others and to the conversation itself — is both generous and generative. It is generous because it makes other people more eloquent. It is, quite literally, a gift. Psychologist Carl Rogers called this 'listening into speech'. When people feel heard, they relax, find it easier to choose their words and say more interesting things. When I speak Spanish, I notice that with some people I speak more fluently than others. The difference is in how they listen to me. The same happens in our mother tongue, but it is more subtle, so we don't notice.

Listening is generative because it creates a field of possibility. That field is present even when no one is talking; indeed, it is *especially* present when no one is talking. This marks live conversation out from text or chat, where there is no shared experience in the gaps between what is said. Just as a tree provides a habitat for wildlife, it is listening that creates a habitat for conversation.

Listening is a physical skill not an abstract idea. My son Mateo, who is a musician, says, 'Listening is about feeling what's right, it is visceral not cognitive, my music suffers when I think too much.' Evelyn Glennie is a world-famous classical percussionist and she is deaf. Her virtuosity is extreme, but everyone listens with more than their ears.

This means you can start with the body. Lean in, literally and metaphorically. Pay attention to your position and posture. Can you listen beyond the words? Can you open yourself up physically and listen with your chest, your belly, your shoulders, your limbs? Julie Batty talks of how, when you are really listening, your skin, fingertips and whole body feel alive.

This isn't about trying to micro-manage specific physical gestures, it is about learning to develop your sensitivity to subtle sensation, sometimes called 'felt-sense'. It goes beyond the intellectual or verbal and involves being present with your bodily sensations and emotions, taking the detail of your own experience seriously.

I have one colleague who reads bodily responses so well that he can tell what I think more quickly than I can myself. Once, after explaining a new idea to me, he quickly pronounced, 'Well, that's obviously one for the birds,' whilst I was still struggling to work out what I thought. When my mind caught up I realised he was right and that I wasn't convinced by the idea. Yet he is a retired businessman not a yoga teacher. Anyone can develop this skill.

Paying attention is intimately related to being present. Theatre director Jerzy Grotowski spent much of his career exploring the idea of presence. His perspective was that to be really present, an actor needs to be able to be fully in touch with their own emotions, thoughts and physical sensations *and* be open and responsive to the energy and reactions of the audience at the same time. It is both at once.

This quality of attention isn't relevant only on stage or in the meditation hall; the same applies in conversation — in order to listen and be present to others, you have to be able to listen and be present to yourself. Conversation both requires and generates presence. When we are really present we disappear: one of the great joys of conversation is losing yourself in it so completely that the sense of being separate dissolves.

This means quiet people are as important to conversation as anyone. If you are really present, you are already participating, you don't always have to be saying something in order to join in. Just sink into your attention to ensure that silence doesn't become absence. Goethe was famous for hosting wonderful conversations yet, apparently, said relatively little. Some of the best conversationalists I know are quiet people, but they are still connected to the conversation. You can physically feel them listening, even online, through the screen. When they do speak up what they say is worth listening to because they have taken the time to think about it. This creates a virtuous circle.

Quieter people can feel pressure to speak up more. It might be better for conversation if louder people felt more pressure to be quiet. So if, like me, you are someone who talks a lot, work on cultivating some quiet as part of your practice. Doing that is often a question of rhythm. In the modern world conversation, like everything else, happens at ever greater speed. Slow down. Pause for a moment and ask yourself whether what you are about to say really needs saying now? Count in your head and see what number you can get to before you speak. If you don't find the moment to say something, the chances are it didn't need saying.

Don't compete. Instead of trying to out-do others, 'find your full stop' and leave gaps for them. This idea, which I find a godsend, comes from actor and trainer Syrus Lowe. It breaks the habit of speaking to fill space and makes you alert to opportunities to stop. Take that further and practise being willing to be interrupted. Whilst speaking, look for the shifts in position and posture that signal someone else's desire to speak, and as soon as you sense them be quick to drop whatever you are saying. Invite interruption. Seek it out instead of blocking it or talking over it.

We all have our own underlying rhythm, but each conversation has a natural rhythm too. With some people I find myself in a pattern of quick exchanges, whereas with others the turn-taking is slower and longer, allowing more complex ideas to be developed. There is no 'right' rhythm, it depends upon the individuals and the circumstances. Even people that meet regularly might have a different rhythm one day compared with another. This will depend upon the subject, their mood or external factors such as the weather or time of day. The natural rhythm of a conversation will also vary as it unfolds, like a piece of music.

You need to be in touch with that. If you aren't you run the risk of talking too much or for too long. That makes it harder for others to join in or offer a contrasting view. It is easy to find yourself moving at the pace of the most impatient person in the room.[2] You might want to check that isn't you.

Talkative people are often the ones who are uncomfortable with silence. We see this in our Yellow groups. In one session, after a long silence, the first person to speak (and he often *was* the first) commented that he had never been part of such a 'reticent' group. Another silence followed before someone else spoke up to challenge that interpretation. 'I don't know about reticent,' she said. 'I was just taking some time to think.'

Silence can be many things. To assume it means people are shy or unwilling to speak is to get ahead of yourself. There is a difference between the silence of boredom and

---

2   I got this idea from facilitator Johnnie Moore.

the silence of rapt attention. Silence can have a palpable energy, it isn't necessarily empty. It is part of a conversation, not separate from it. It allows you to see what comes to mind. Your thoughts might wander outwards and find new ideas to bring into the conversation, or you might go inwards and notice how you feel about what has been said. As Susan Scott puts it, 'Silence allows us to scan our hearts and heads for ground truths.' Quiet can do a lot of work. It creates what the ancient Greeks (and more recently Gestalt psychologists) describe as 'the fertile void'.

Most of our conversations would be improved by more quiet or silence, not less. So when there is some silence, don't race to fill it just because it makes you uncomfortable. Get curious about it. Assume the silence has something to say and see if you can sense what that is. Reframe it as 'thinking time'. With practice you can become more comfortable with silence and better able to read it. Whisper it softly, but the capacity to be quiet is one that is worth developing.

Small talk

Small talk gets a bad rap. It has an awkwardness all of its own. I sometimes feel as if I have nothing to say or can't stop blabbering or both at once. This isn't surprising. What others make of us matters, so when we first start to talk with someone, we are fumbling around whilst the stakes are high.

Some people seem to think that all conversation is small talk, that there is nothing else. Others have a kind of disdain for the trivial and boast that 'I don't do small talk'. At a conference, before a break, I heard a host urge people to 'get beyond the small talk', implying that such frivolity is wasteful and ought to be beneath you.

But nevertheless it plays an important role. You get a sense of that when it is dispensed with. I once attended a party with cast, crew and VIPs before a premiere at the Berlin International Film Festival. A friend of mine was one of the dignitaries and I went along for the ride. When she was whisked off to talk to the star of the movie, a glamorous woman, dressed (like everyone else) completely in black, strode up and, by way of introduction, said, 'I'm the director's wife. Who are you?' When I told her I was simply accompanying my friend, she turned tail and, without another word, went to find someone else talk to.

Small talk occupies the space between nothing and something. It is a kind of departure lounge for conversation, providing a space in which you can begin to coordinate the subtle complexities of speech and social interaction — timing and rhythm, power and status, commonality and difference, and so on. It is there to help us work out how, in this particular conversation, we are going to dance together. It reminds me of the rasping hiss of an old modem connecting. It may sound terrible, but it is a necessary prelude, prior to the exchange of meaningful information. Dogs sniff around. Modems handshake. We do small talk.

The point is the transition. Small talk is only there to get you somewhere else. But if we get nervous or try too hard, we get stuck in it and fall into a pattern of being competitive and judgemental. The Swedish call it 'cold talk' (*kallsnack*) not small talk. This captures the chilly nature of talk that doesn't go anywhere.

I think of this as 'dead talk' not small talk. I mention Mallorca, you raise me the Maldives. I recall bumping into David Beckham, you tell me about the time you met the Queen. The novelist Nick Hornby describes this 'you first, then me' pattern as the 'lavatory of conversation, where there is only room for one at a time'. No field is created and nothing new appears. It is a hollow kind of exchange that feels awkward and leads nowhere.

However, you can get through it almost immediately. For example, I first met Dr Neil Randhawa in the queue for tea at the Do Lectures in 2011. I asked him what he did. 'I am a doctor,' he said, 'but I told my colleagues I was going mountain biking, they wouldn't understand all this.' That single phrase, which went further than was necessary (making it into a 'doorknob'), catapulted us through the small talk and into a fascinating conversation and friendship, that more than a decade later is still going strong.

Basketball coach Phil Jackson once said, 'Not only is there more to life than basketball, there's a lot more to basketball than basketball.' Things that sound trivial often have more to them than meets the eye. To pick that up you have to pay attention to when people light up or where they pause. Be interested in that rather than trying to be interesting. Assume you have something to learn from everyone and try to discover what it might be. That will draw you in, the other person will feel it and the conversation will warm up.

There are some set phrases that can help in common situations, for example, when you find yourself asking one of the staples of small talk: 'What do you do?' Rather than try to avoid it, which can feel forced or strange, think about how you follow it up. For example:

ME: 'So what do you do?'
ROWAN: 'I am a gerontologist, specialised in Alzheimer's.'
ME: *'That must be hard...'*

'That must be hard' is a rare 'killer phrase'. Whatever Rowan says, it works. It draws something out — in this case I learned how, with Alzheimer's patients, it is helpful to talk less and be more direct because they have trouble processing information (making it a particular cultural problem in England, where we are often indirect).

Notice that the phrase 'that must be hard' isn't a question at all but a statement that invites a response. It sees the other person and affirms something positive (even flattering) about them whilst giving them freedom to respond how they want. There is no stock answer so what they say will be fresh.

It works whether they are a banker, doctor, fireman, baker, astronaut, shepherd, priest, chocolatier, life coach, bullfighter or special-needs classroom assistant.[3] If they don't have a job at all and say, 'I don't do anything,' then it really works — for a different reason, perhaps, but it still works. Even if they disagree ('Actually, being a chocolatier is really easy') the conversation is already moving.

The podcaster Joe Rogan often uses the phrase 'that reminds me of...' If you have the kind of magpie mind that is always picking up shiny nuggets then 'that reminds me of...' can be a useful bridge to something new. But if you don't naturally make such connections, simply saying, 'That reminds me of...' and dredging up a memory is unlikely to help.

There are times when the conversation isn't meant to go anywhere (or you don't want it to). In rural Spain some of the exchanges I have are almost rituals. We comment about the drought (there's always a drought) and ask after the kids. But these are extended greetings not a failed

---

3   I borrowed this list from a sketch by Armstrong and Miller entitled 'What Do I Actually Do?' Look it up. It's hilarious.

attempt at conversation. If you decide you don't want the conversation to progress, you can choose to stay in lavatory conversation until you find the moment to visit the actual lavatory, as a literal and metaphorical way out.

Small talk shows up many of the patterns of conversation I have been talking about in miniature. You need to offer something to the other person. You need to 'see' them by hearing them. It doesn't help to sound off about yourself or to incessantly grill other people. Don't just ask questions. Don't just make statements. Be patient. Don't expect too much. Look for doorknobs to drop in or pull on.

Conversation is rich precisely because it is so sensitive to context. The conditions matter as much as the individuals (something we will explore more in Chapter 4). Everyone struggles at times. Yet cultivate a few simple practices and small talk can quickly turn into something bigger (or deeper). An everyday miracle can emerge out of quite ordinary things.

If at first you don't succeed, give up and try something else. Having a practice means you can always begin again. Above all, forget the idea of having a script. Conversation is a wonderful, unending, unfolding improvisation, which is where we are going to look next for inspiration.

Most of our conversations would be improved by more quiet or silence, not less. So when there is some silence, don't race to fill it just because it makes you uncomfortable. Get curious about it.

DO

4
Improvised
conversation

A conversation isn't scripted. If it were there would be little point in having it. The very essence of conversation is that it is a response, to a response, to a response, and so on. It is this responsiveness that means conversation is alive. This plays out not just in the moment but over extended periods of time — I might respond to something that was said a moment, a week or a year ago (this 'reincorporation' is something I will come back to later).

The way we respond depends upon the particulars of who we are — on our own character, experience or perspective. We each bring something to the conversation that no one else does and together create something no one could alone. This finely grained, branching tree of responses, to responses, to responses, is why you never know which path a conversation will take.

There is joy in this uncertainty. It creates surprise and delight. It gives birth to new ideas and possibilities. If we knew everything that was going to happen in advance, life would be insufferably flat and dull, but uncertainty also makes us nervous.

Navigating uncertainty without a script means cultivating the ability to improvise. You are good at this already —

far better than you realise. You don't have a script for your life (no one does) and yet, one way or another, you are able to cope with the complexity you face. You may not think of it as such, but your life as a whole is a towering improvisation — the elements you determine and control yourself are few. Even so, you do more than just get by; you are able, sometimes at least, to thrive and prosper.

Nowhere is this more obvious than in conversation. Every conversation is a responsive, adaptive dance. You don't know what others will say or even what you will say yourself. Happily for us there is an existing body of knowledge, language and practice that was developed by improvisers in the theatre, which maps beautifully onto conversation. This gives us a ready-made set of tools and practices to pilfer, which can help us become more skilled at navigating the uncertainty and unpredictability inherent in conversation.

At the heart of this is a simple model. It is incomplete and flawed, as all models are, but that doesn't stop it being useful. If you have read *Do Improvise* you will recognise it and if you haven't, never mind, it is quick to explain and easy to understand.

It is based on three simple and interconnected practices. They are: notice more, let go and use everything.

These practices can also be phrased as questions:

— What else could I **notice**?

— What could I **let go** of (or loosen my grip on)?

— Whatever I have, how can I **use** it?

Each one leads to the others, so you can start anywhere.

Notice more

'Noticing more' is one way to 'pay attention to how you pay attention'. The practice of 'noticing more' draws your attention to what is actually happening right now in the conversation, including what you are sensing or feeling, which is useful and important information.

The mantra 'notice more' is particularly useful when a conversation feels stuck or awkward. If you are scrambling around in your own head, looking for something clever to say, or trying to remember something from a list, it takes you out of the moment and you are distanced, even absent, from the conversation. Other people will feel that. Instead, if you lean into your senses in an attempt to notice more, that helps make you present, which people will also feel.

Looking for something to use is a creative act. However familiar the surroundings there is always more to notice. Look and you will find. You might notice a fleeting smile or frown on someone's face. You might notice how people have different rhythms within the conversation and adapt to them. You might notice your own inner sensations and realise you aren't as uncomfortable with the silence as you assumed. The ultimate conversation starter is to use what you have, not look somewhere else.

Even online there is a lot to notice. Gary Hirsch, with whom I founded an improv-based consultancy, invented a whole genre of games that revolve around noticing what is in the background of someone's screen and using those observations to start conversations. With so many people working from home, there are 'offers' everywhere. Noticing a map on the wall might start a conversation about a life-changing journey that would otherwise have remained unmentioned. When you don't know what to do to get a conversation going, start with what you notice.

The improvisational maxim 'obvious is good' is one way to do this. What is obvious to you may not be obvious to someone else, so just use that. It might be all you need to do. This stops you trying too hard. People are delighted when someone uses what is right in front of them. When your obvious meets my obvious we get something new. Originality and discovery lie in the combinations not individual contributions, so you need to create a conversational climate where different contributions connect and add up, not cancel each other out or compete.

Let go

For that to happen, you have to let go. Letting go is a fabulous practice for conversation because we often come at it with so much 'wanting'. We want to achieve a result or reach an outcome we have already settled on. We want to 'get' people to agree with us, or convince them of our worth. Or we want to show we are good at conversation.

When we wind ourselves up in a web of wants, we hobble any possibility of a proper conversation before it even gets going. Often we want to impress people. Over the course of ten years, the Brazilian journalist Leila Ferreira had conversations with hundreds of people — some famous, some ordinary — on her television show. On one occasion her guest was an eminent psychologist. The two of them were enjoying a lively conversation until the cameras started rolling, whereupon he became a different person, talking only about his own achievements and book sales. Leila stopped the interview and asked him to let go of trying to impress people and talk as he had been before the filming began. She knew that the show worked because the conversations were natural.

We can all fall into this trap, even without the cameras. We are social creatures, so we care about what others think of us. Ironically, our attempts to impress are more likely to make the conversation stilted not fluent. When conversation becomes a status game, it isn't really conversation at all, it is a jousting match. Don't rise to the bait, let that go.

The language itself gives us a clue here. We talk of 'falling' or 'dropping' into a conversation. To do that you have to let go of having a detailed idea of where you want it to go. At the events I host, letting go of specific goals and objectives makes it highly likely something of value will emerge — I just don't know what it will be in advance. Which is part of the fun.

Letting go might be the best way to get what you really want anyway. Let go of trying to impress people and they might be more impressed. Let people have their own say and they might end up agreeing with you. Let go of arriving at a particular destination and you might discover somewhere more interesting. As the writer George Saunders says, 'Conversations go badly because we so desperately want them to go well.'

Letting go of your agenda expands the field of conversation and allows space for things you can't anticipate. In a recent conversation with Jason Trew (the US Air Force colonel I mentioned earlier), a comment about Salisbury Cathedral led to a conversation about scaffolding and flexible structures. Jason referred to the work of a German academic, Claus Jacobs, which uses Lego to develop strategy. As it happens, Claus is a friend of mine and by pure chance he was staying with me at the time, so I invited him to join the conversation. The connections aren't always as neat as this, but the sideways ramble is often fruitful. You can't be sure something good will happen, but if you don't ever let go, you can be sure that it won't. Which is a waste.

Letting go is about not becoming attached to a particular path or outcome. As a professional journalist, Leila prepares meticulously before she talks with someone; however, when she is with them, she lets all the preparation go, so that she can be present to the person she is with. It is important, she says, 'not to go out with ready-made answers, but to hang on to the questions'. This is what creates the space for a field of conversation rather than 'a game of verbal ping-pong'. Jason Trew agrees. He says, 'When you have an answer you close off all the questions.' A conversation is not so much a series of questions and answers, but, like jazz, a matter of call and response that can develop in ways none of the players anticipate.

Hold plans, agendas and expectations lightly. Be willing to venture into territory you are unfamiliar with. We often hide behind our occupations — a doctor talks only about medicine or a pilot about aviation. Tethering a conversation within the bounds of your expertise doesn't allow for exploration or discovery. Letting go is liberating.

Letting go also helps you listen. We all know how important that is in conversation, but the idea of 'listening better' is too vague to act upon. Improvisers have a useful practice here. They focus on being changed by what they hear from others. Enter a conversation with this in mind and it forces you to listen: if you don't, you won't know how to be changed.

There are plenty of things you can practise letting go of in conversation: an agenda, a belief, an assumption, even part of your identity. You might let go of wanting to sound clever, look good or be right; or the idea that you always have to be productive. Let go of the idea of conversation as combat and focus on how much you can learn, not who knows most. Let go of what you expect to happen next. If you want to have more intimate conversations you might need to let go of being too careful. You might let go of the idea of control (of yourself, others or the conversation itself). Or you might let go of having an opinion and allow yourself not to know.

It is a long list, but you don't have to let go of everything at once. Letting go is not about becoming passive or inert, it is about introducing some play into a conversation — room to move or space to create. It encourages you to put down some of the burden that you carry. Tim Yearsley, whose job is to engage students and young adults in conversation, talks of approaching a conversation 'clean and empty'. This allows for obliquity, for the tangents and digressions that can enrich the conversation. It shifts you from a two-dimensional linear perspective, where you try to reach a particular point, to a three-dimensional one, where the conversation is able to expand in any direction. Wandering and wondering go together.

Use everything

The third practice, 'use everything', is intertwined with the first two. Author and leadership coach Susan Scott talks of the importance of coming into a 'fierce' conversation 'with empty hands, bring nothing but yourself'. But of course, if you bring yourself that is not nothing. You contain 'multitudes', so any and every aspect of your experience is something you can use. That includes your energy, feelings and sensations (and the body that bears them) as well as facts, information or experience.

Emotion is data too. This doesn't mean every conversation has to be 'touchy-feely' but a good conversation is always informed by sensation and feeling. Reason alone won't tell you what you are curious about, puzzled by or interested in.

Feelings give you a different kind of information and learning to access your own sensations and feelings is a practice in itself. Just because they are in your body, doesn't mean that you are automatically in touch with them — you have to develop your own sensitivity.

To 'use everything' is to reframe things that might normally be labelled as mistakes, errors or shortcomings as things you can use. Everything is grist for the mill. It is a reminder to pay attention beyond the words: to gesture, energy, movement, tone, rhythm, pace, pause, silence and so on. There is more to work with than what is said. Allow yourself to be guided by the 'how' as well as the 'what'.

Remember you have a body. A body that speaks volumes without words. Get interested in how you use it in conversation and explore the opportunities it affords you. Play around with posture, position, gesture. What happens — to you or to others — when you lean forward or lean back? When you incline your head? When you sit still? When you use expansive gestures? When you clench your jaw, or shoulders (or relax them)? This isn't about playing a role, it is about becoming aware of the effects of how you hold yourself in conversation, so that you can use more of yourself, more consciously.

You can even use what you don't know. Say 'I don't know' more often and — instead of pretending, apologising or retreating from the conversation — ask more questions. Which leads us back to letting go again. Let go of the idea that you need to be an expert or have an opinion about everything and you will learn more.

Be generous

At the intersection of the three circles in the diagram is a practice that ties them together: 'everything is an offer'. This simply means that anything can be taken and used. In conversation this practice works in two complementary ways, both of them generous.

Think about the offers you make. Are you making simple, clear, explicit offers? This includes but isn't limited to what you say. A nod, a gesture, a sound or a movement can also be an offer, as could an unfinished sentence. To make more offers doesn't necessarily imply speaking more, or for longer, you could just say 'so...' and see what that sparks off. But check you are doing and saying things that give other people something to work with. Can you make bolder, clearer offers?

Second, think about how you receive offers. Be generous there too. You can choose to use anything, even what doesn't happen, as an offer. If someone else is unresponsive, see it as an offer, and ask yourself what you can do with that. You might let go of making a judgement about what is going on for them, and instead ask them. You might respond to silence by settling into silence yourself, rather than trying to jolly things along. It is up to you how you use it, but if you are willing to see anything as an offer, it becomes one.

This attitude makes you humble as well as generous and puts you in service of the conversation, not your own ego. Whatever happens (or doesn't), whatever is said (or not said), devote your energy to looking for a way to use it. This is the ultimate version of 'use everything'. Do this and there will be flow in the conversation. It may well flow in a direction you didn't expect, but that can be the most delightful thing of all.

The offer funnel

One of the basic challenges of conversation is how much to say — when to speak up and when to sit back. This will always depend upon the particulars of the situation as well as your own personality and style, so there are no simple answers here, but there is an improv tool that you can use to help you think about what to do. It is called 'The Offer Funnel'. It looks like this:

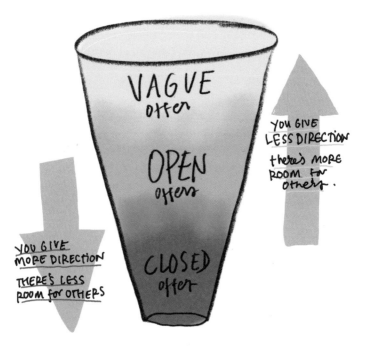

At the top are 'vague' offers, in the middle are 'open' offers and at the bottom, in the narrow part of the funnel, are 'closed' offers.

Vague offers don't have much information in them. You don't say much and aren't very precise or specific. This allows others the freedom to take the conversation in many different directions. Vague offers are useful to get things going or in a 'conversation of possibility'. You don't have to work hard to craft a vague offer. The 'so...' I mentioned earlier is about as vague an offer as you can get. When I did qualitative research I learned that when I didn't know what to say next, this was really useful. As long as I was happy to sit with a few moments of silence it always got a response, often a highly productive one.

Open offers, which sit in the middle of the funnel, have more information in them but still give people room for manoeuvre. Tracey Camilleri's 'half-finished sentences' fit here. They could be questions or statements. For example, just yesterday I made the open offer to my friend Nick Parker that I would like to run a writing workshop with him. That begins to shape our conversation but still leaves a lot to talk about (when, where, why, how long it might be, what we might do and so on). Open offers are useful in the midst of conversation and enable co-creation, where responsibility is shared. A doorknob is a particularly fruity kind of open offer.

A closed offer, as you would expect, is one that narrows down the possible responses to a small number of alternatives, often 'yes' or 'no'. For example: 'That feels to me like an end.' Closed offers lean heavily in one direction. They are useful to conclude or close, or in a 'conversation for action' where you need to make decisions.

This framework enables you to see the ebb and flow of a conversation as it unfolds and to identify what is needed.

It won't tell you what to say, but can help you to see what *kind* of contribution would help the conversation at that point. If you are beginning, or early in a process, use vague or open offers. If you want to end, move down the funnel and make closed offers. Often conversations will yo-yo up and down as they move through different phases.

Colour and advance

In conversation, you sometimes get lost in the weeds. At other times you aren't engaged and become disconnected emotionally. Improvisers have some language that can help you spot these moments and give you something to do about them. They use the words 'colour' and 'advance' in a particular way. 'Colour' means detail, texture or description. 'Advance' is anything that creates action or change. In conversation, colour means going deeper into what is already there: advance means going further and getting to something new. A good conversation needs an ebb and flow between 'colour' and 'advance'.

If the conversation is all colour it feels slow and heavy. If it is all advance, there may be a lot of crash-bang-wallop, but there is little reason to care about what is being said. Looking through this lens gives you another way to frame a conversation. Is it racing ahead without any depth? Or is it mired in detail and in desperate need of impetus and movement?

This tool will also tell you something about yourself. In conversation, most of us have a natural preference for one or the other. Armed with the language of 'colour' and 'advance', ask yourself what your own preferences are and check whether you are serving them, rather than the conversation. Are you always adding colour when others want to move on? Are you racing ahead, when others want to dwell on something? You may have a different style at home or at work, but if you are honest with yourself, you will readily identify your own leanings.

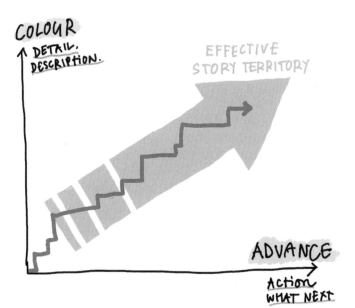

Routines

Those leanings can become what improvisers call a 'routine'. A routine, in this context, is a repeated pattern of behaviour and it is another useful term we can use to look at conversation. Action is created by interrupting a routine, so you can use that idea in a conversation that feels stuck.

Start by looking for conversational routines. They might be obvious — people might literally be saying the same things over and over. Or it could be a routine in the roles — one person speaking a lot and another staying quiet. Or a habitual pattern in what you talk about or where you meet. Once you spot these you have the chance to interrupt them deliberately. You could introduce something new or invite reflection by calling out that the conversation is going in circles. If you talk a lot, break that routine for a bit by staying quiet. If you are quiet, break it by speaking up. Looking for routines draws you into the conversation. It invites you into the core practice of noticing more, then letting go — by looking for an established pattern then interrupting it.

Be interested, not interesting

It was the essayist William Hazlitt who said: 'Whatever interests is interesting' (something I touched on in the previous chapter). On stage, improvisers focus on being interested, not interesting. An audience finds this engaging. In conversation don't try and second-guess what is 'interesting' to others, pay attention to what you are interested in, which means reading your own bodily responses and sensations. What is there in the conversation that brings you alive? What is arising for you? Go there.

Status

I hate it when a conversation becomes a 'tennis match' —
a series of rapid exchanges around status. I find it boring
and competitive. For me, and many of the people I
interviewed for this book, this competitiveness is part of
what makes small talk small (or cold, to use the Swedish
term *kallsnack* again).

A conversation is less fluent and creative when the
same people always dominate. Improvisers have the
idea that status is something you can play around with.
Conversation becomes more engaging when people take
turns holding a position of power and are able to dance
between high and low status.

How you say something can change your status.
Being definitive, concise and clear raises it, for example,
saying: 'What is really happening here is...'

Body language has a huge effect — keeping your head
still and using an even tone also raises status.

To lower your status, express doubt or uncertainty.
For example, 'Is it just me, or...' Move or fidget, touch
your head or vary the volume you speak at, and it lowers
your status.

Again, you can start to use this practice simply by
noticing what your normal tendency is in conversation.
Are you always trying to play high? That can bring clarity
but if you always play high it will exclude others. Or do you
default to a humble, low-status position? If so, then you
will be more inclusive but your views might be dismissed
or ignored. Whatever your style, play around with it and
see what happens. Looking at the pattern of status in a
conversation (either during or afterwards) will also shed
some light on why it was satisfying (or dissatisfying).

Once you see this, a conversation never looks the same again — looking at status shifts can become addictive.[1] But you don't need to go into such depth; the simple idea that status is something to play around with can enrich, or unlock, your conversation.

Reincorporation

I mentioned reincorporation earlier and by recalling it now I am doing it. Reincorporation means bringing something back from earlier in the story. It is satisfying because it shows that someone has been paying attention over an extended period and because it connects different elements of a conversation (or narrative).

Understanding this reminds you that in a conversation you don't always have to add something new to weave a conversation together. Just pay attention to what is already there. That won't work if you haven't listened, so it also encourages you to listen. It is useful if you want to reach a conclusion — you can reach an end by looping back.

Beyond the specific practices and tools, the spirit that improvisers bring to their work is also a gift for conversation. Improvisers, (on stage at least) are generous to each other. They look after themselves by looking after others and they are playful. Play isn't just fun, it makes more things possible, stops you taking yourself too seriously and gives you new perspectives.

If you could script your conversations, how interesting would that be? A script means you only say things you

---

1   There is more detail on this in *Do Improvise* and, for the really curious, a whole chapter on it in my earlier book *Everything's an Offer*.

have already thought of. There would be nothing new. No discovery, no new connections, no insights, no moments of revelation.

The delights of conversation do not depend upon being in command or control — of yourself, others or the conversation. Instead of working ever harder trying to engineer things to be the way you think you want them, you can focus on a few simple practices and enjoy the unexpected delights that emerge from an infinite game.

5
**To host
and to hold**

You have a different conversation at a boardroom table than you do at a dining table; or with no table at all; or sitting round a fire; or on a walk. Context matters. The space you are in, how you are arranged within it, time of day, time pressure (or lack of it), start point, presence (or absence) of food and drink and so on, all make a difference. There are many ingredients in the mix.

This gives you another place to act. Put benches in the square, literally or metaphorically, and people are more likely to sit and talk. We have a hand in how we hold conversation. Sometimes this is explicit — it might be part of your job to choose the space or book time in the calendar — but even if you have no formal responsibility you can still influence the setting. You can sit somewhere else, rearrange the chairs or offer people a drink.[1] How you show up will affect how others behave, particularly if you are someone they respect or care about.

---

1   If you are English this is likely to be tea. It seems that English people are largely incapable of having a conversation without it. Even my eldest son, who is only half English, is fond of saying: 'A conversation is always better with tea.'

If you understand the power of framing, it helps you shape a conversation. When I arrived at Nick's house a few nights back he explicitly gave me a choice: 'Tea or whisky, kitchen or fire pit?' he asked. That simple question mapped out a range of different possibilities (we went for tea in the fire pit).

When you host a party you know instinctively that the setting matters, so you make sure there is enough food and drink, rearrange the furniture, make choices about lighting and music and think about where people will leave their coats. Convening a conversation is similar. In fact, sometimes the parallel is almost literal. When making a film, director David Keating regards 'dinner as a secret weapon'. To create the space for a conversation with an actor or technician he will take them out to dinner. This isn't about flattery or luxury. A meal is a highly nuanced container that affords you lots of options — you could choose a sandwich bar or a Michelin-starred restaurant depending on what you are after. Another film director, Garry Marshall (of *Pretty Woman* fame), took the idea even further. It was said of him that: 'He didn't so much direct a movie, as host it.'

Context has a particularly strong effect when no one thinks about it, which is one reason why so many meetings are deathly. If you book the same old meeting room, you are likely to have the same old conversation. If that's what you want, fine, but if you want something new or different then it's a problem. It is even worse online, where the experience is so much thinner than in person. You can have great conversations online, but creating the conditions for that requires extra care and attention not less (see page 85, 'In the beginning').

This doesn't mean that by designing the context you can control the outcome any more than you can control what people do or say at a party. Quite the opposite, in fact. If you set up a conversation well, you will get a wealth of responses you couldn't predict, but that is a good thing.

The right setting helps people listen better and open up more; they give more to the conversation and get more from it. The bedrock is to create an atmosphere of safety, trust and intimacy, which is why kitchens are such a good place for conversation. There is no formula for this, you can have 'pop-up rules' that only apply to a particular conversation, and there are many variations you can play around with. Most of them don't take much work, effort or money. First, there are two basic questions to ask:

— **What kind of conversation is this?**
— **Who is participating?**

You may have some say in these or they may be givens. After that, you simply make choices about four practical things, which are:

— **How you use physical space**
— **How you structure the time**
— **The inputs** (materials, props or other stimuli)
— **How you show up**

That's it. Let's have a look at each of these in turn. The examples I use come more from the world of work, where we do more explicit convening, but it is also relevant at home, just more subtle.

What kind of conversation is it?

First, think about the *kind* of conversation you want.
Are you trying to take a decision, explore different options
or discover something new? Is energy or reflection more
important? Do you want to deepen or widen; connect or
disentangle? To use Fernando Flores' terms, do you want a
conversation for understanding, possibility or relationship?
Most conversations ebb and flow between one kind and
another but it helps to identify what is primary.

Who do you invite?

Conversation only works at human scale. Otherwise you
cannot create trust and intimacy. Intimacy here doesn't
mean sharing personal secrets but being able to sense the
other people in the conversation. When people talk of
having 'a national conversation' it is a metaphor — a whole
country cannot sit down to talk.

However, a conversation also needs enough difference
to provide variety. Variety is about personal styles and
temperaments as well as differences in age, experience,
culture, ethnicity and sexual orientation. Regardless of
where people are from, if everyone in the room has an MBA
you won't necessarily get much variety in how they think.

There is a creative tension between intimacy and
variety but in conversation small really is beautiful, so
rein in the temptation to include people without good
reason. Don't add people for appearances' sake, to make
them feel wanted or 'just in case'. If you 'over-include' the
conversation is more likely to be shallow.

There are no hard-and-fast rules or absolute numbers,
but beyond a certain threshold every person you add

diminishes the chances of a good conversation, not just a little, but dramatically. What does that mean in practice? Priya Parker, in *The Art of Gathering*, suggests you can't really have a conversation with more than thirty. I am more drastic. In my experience once you get into double figures things start to change. When our local film club was a dozen people or less, we used to have fascinating conversations all the time. Now it is twenty or more, we rarely do.

Take this seriously. If you have to have a big group, then you will need to manage expectations as well as the conversation itself. You simply won't get the same kind of open, deep, fluid conversation you would with a smaller group. Everyday miracles can't be scaled. The field can't be stretched too thin.

Using 'break-out' groups is a common response to this but it doesn't solve the problem, it re-creates it. Break-out groups give people more chance to speak, but only by fragmenting the conversation into separate shards which are hard to put together again. This is why the reporting back on small groups is so often dreadful.

When it comes to scale, err on the side of small. In the long run, a larger number of smaller conversations will be more effective than fewer large ones. I had one client who, in place of a three-day annual conference with all her staff, spoke to them individually or in small groups for twenty minutes or so during the course of the year. When she compared the total time spent on each approach, there wasn't much difference. But she received far more useful information and employees were far more engaged when she spoke with them directly.

Physical space

The physical space you use is more than a practical issue, it also has symbolic value. It will affect how people feel, how they listen to each other and what they say. This isn't just about cheap or expensive. A luxurious hotel in sumptuous grounds may impress people, but it may also put them on their 'best behaviour'. If what you are after is frank, open dialogue such a space can work against you. An actor I spoke to said that 'we used to have better rehearsals in a scruffy room above a pub, than in a purpose-built space at the Royal Shakespeare Company'. The pub encouraged the rough conversations needed in rehearsal, whereas the smart new room inhibited them. However, if you are always in a scruffy pub, you might be inspired by somewhere beautiful. No option is good or bad in its own right, it depends on what you want.

On the leadership programmes in Oxford we use a wealth of different settings in deliberate ways: everything from a brutalist concrete building outside the ring road to the woods it is set in, the coffee station, an ornate college chapel, the streets of the medieval city and the bus ride that takes us there. We change the layout of the dining room, the size and shape of the tables and the kind of food we serve day by day to suit our purposes. We design the spaces as much as the sessions because we want to create a coral reef for conversation, with lots of different niches that different kinds of conversation can inhabit.

Don't assume you just need room to sit everyone in a chair at a table — and don't take what a venue says about how many people fit in a space at face value. Small rooms concentrate the mind, large ones expand it. Think about the furniture you need or want to get rid of, the light, access to the outdoors. Notice the qualities of the building (old or new, smart or scruffy, efficient or eccentric) and ask yourself how you can use them to support the kind of conversation you want.

Brand consultancy eatbigfish will often choose a photographic studio for their strategy workshops — the (literally) blank backdrop subtly suggests anything can be considered, the space can be set in many ways and studios are good at getting hold of all sorts of props or materials, quickly. Thus the space prefigures the kind of conversation that a brand reconsidering its future needs to have.

The effects of space can be far-reaching. A speechwriter told me that whilst the House of Lords is being restored, they have moved temporarily into another building and this has changed the kind of conversations they have. His conclusion was that our political discourse is shaped by the adversarial benches of Parliament's historic home.

Tables and chairs

Don't just think about space when you are hiring a venue or moving to a new building. It matters just as much in the everyday environment. At home and at work you have a panorama of different spaces and you can vary how you use them. Is this conversation one for the kitchen or the lounge? The boardroom or the water cooler? How might you arrange that space?

Details matter. We are sensitive to small differences, even if we aren't conscious of them. In his film *American Beauty*, director Sam Mendes wanted to make a dinner scene feel awkward, so he deliberately used a table that was too big. When that happened to me at a wedding it felt dreadful — it was hard to connect with anyone because they were a little bit too far away. Physical distance creates emotional distance. If family members always sit in the same seats to eat, the relationships are likely to mirror the physical set-up and become fixed. If you want to weave everyone together, why not move them around, instead of having set places?

At work, if you set chairs in a circle with no table at all, it will suggest a confessional kind of conversation, so expect someone to make a quip about therapy. Set the chairs in pairs facing each other and you create a vehicle for 'speed dating' — multiple, simultaneous, iterated pair conversations. Set the pairs in a line and it suggests there is a progression from one point to another. Put them in concentric circles and it feels like you are rotating through a whole. A standing meeting, with no chairs at all, implies a focus on efficiency and speed. And so on.

These physical cues may seem trivial but the effects are potent. They are a signal, priming people as they arrive and shaping their responses as the conversation unfolds. They don't determine the dialogue but they do set the stage, so set it in a way you think will be helpful.

Shoulder to shoulder vs face to face

For example, talking shoulder to shoulder or face to face are different. You either look out at something else, or you look at each other. It is said that women prefer face-to-face conversation and men prefer 'shoulder to shoulder'. Whoever you are, it is useful to understand that even in a pair, you have options. You could choose to have a conversation with someone whilst walking, washing up, or on a car journey.

Car journeys are a great space for conversation. They are (necessarily) shoulder to shoulder. They allow for silence and quiet. What you see out the window provides some gentle stimulus and because you aren't facing each other, it can be easier to say certain things. Looking into a fire has similar qualities.

By contrast, facing someone across a table, you can give them your undivided attention. You could use this to show that you are 100 per cent there for them or to grill them about something they are avoiding — the set-up will help either. Sitting across the corner of a table is another option, partway between.

In a workshop, a group version of this is 'wall' vs 'tabletop'. Stick material on a wall and people are looking at it together (shoulder to shoulder). The material is at a distance and is out of arm's reach, so it isn't easy to reconfigure. If the ideas are on a tabletop, people are facing each other and the material can easily be shuffled. If you want to reach an agreement, the arrangement on the wall might work better. If you want to keep things fluid, the tabletop version might be the one to plump for.

You can make considered choices about where to place people. It only takes a little thought but it makes a big difference.

Space as a constraint

You can use space as a constraint. For example, I was recently hosting an in-person gathering to discuss the future of a business, which suggested a small, intimate conversation. Yet we also wanted to give everyone the chance to participate — and there were 25 people there.

We chose a space around a fireplace with only five seats, which limited how many people could be there at any one moment. But we added a rule that you could come and go. If a space was free you could join at any time. If you wanted to leave, you could. If a space wasn't free, you could tap someone on the shoulder and they would vacate their seat. How you organise things in space can intersect with how you organise them in time.

Time

Time is the second thing to think about. A morning conversation will feel more focused than an afternoon or evening one. A late-night conversation has a flavour and a quality all of its own (which is one reason why kids love sleepovers). Don't assume it makes no difference. It isn't just a practical choice.

As well as time of day, there is the question of timing. Timing is as important to conversation as it is to music. Pace and rhythm, duration and frequency, iteration and repetition, beginnings and endings; these are all things you can work with.

In the beginning

Beginnings matter. Which is (partly) why we feel nervous about small talk. How you start affects how you go on, something complexity scientists call 'sensitivity to initial conditions'. Given that, don't rush the beginning, especially when you are keen to get on. Conversations are not linear. Starting gently pays off later.

People need to settle into a conversation, to feel how they are (or *who* they are) in this company. Even for a family or an established team, this is important: however well they know each other, they have never been in this particular moment before. Be patient. Though it may feel slow, it need not take long and if you don't pay attention to how the conversation begins, it is unlikely to pick up pace (or depth) as it unfolds. More haste less speed.

There is an art to ushering people aboard, particularly online. Over the last three years, by hosting hundreds of groups online for Yellow, I have learned a lot about beginnings, so I am going to use that as an example. It gives you a flavour of how much is going on at the beginning of a conversation and how many levels you can work on.

Alex and I are always online first and as soon as the first person joins we let go of the practical mode we have been in and become curious and playful. We show and share what we are feeling and allow ourselves to be a bit silly, which invites participants to do likewise. How we show up ourselves (which we will get to shortly) sets the tone.

There is an element of ritual. Once everyone has arrived, I ask Alex, 'What check-in question do you have for us today?' This repeated piece of structure is a threshold, which tips us into the formal beginning. Alex has been on the lookout for something to use during the chit-chat. He will choose a question based on something one of them has said, which 'sees' them. That might be as obvious as using a comment about the weather to ask, 'What is your internal weather today?' When he can't immediately find anything, he is happy to show the struggle rather than try to appear slick.

After everyone has responded (including us) we allow a beat for the participants to share anything that is weighing on their minds — e.g. that their dog has just died or their firm is laying people off. Often, no one has anything to say, but holding the silence for a few seconds makes a difference: empty space is useful structure. Only then do we frame what we aim to do that day. Any practical 'housekeeping' stuff, we save for the end.

There are times when we let the conversation follow something that appears during this beginning, abandoning what we had planned. When we do that, it isn't random or lazy, it is because we pick up that people have energy for whatever it is.

Whether you are working online or in person, ask yourself what kind of beginnings suits your purposes? What do you structure in advance and where do you give yourself space to respond to others? Where are you when people arrive? Do you stand, or sit, or greet them by the door, or keep your distance (or arrive after they do)? What mood do you want? What energy do you embody? Do you start with a question, a statement, a game, a gesture, a blessing or some silent reflection (a practice used at Brockwood Park School near Winchester to allow students to 'arrive' from their previous lesson). There are a thousand things you could do, including the thing you normally do. You don't always have to be inventive, so the normal thing might be fine, but whatever you do, take the trouble to choose consciously. Start as you mean to go on.

Duration

The boundaries you set in time create both a limit and an expectation. A short time with a crisp boundary (or 'hard stop' as it is sometimes called) provides a sharp focus, with little space for tangents or exploration. Is that what you want? Or would you prefer a more open conversation, in which case you would use extended time lengths and fuzzier boundaries.

Many of the best conversations often aren't scheduled at all, but emerge on their own. Which means developing a sensitivity rather than a plan. Here the improv practice comes in handy. You have to notice that a conversation worth having is appearing and be willing to let go of whatever else you are doing to make space for it. Once you tip into it, then you can think if you want to sit on a nearby bench, keep walking, settle in a room or whatever. You can still craft the setting on the fly.

What is the rhythm of conversation that you are looking for? A leadership development group I belong to, which includes people in big jobs, meets once a month. Aiming for more would lead to cancellations and the whole thing would unravel. Think about what is realistic and how much continuity matters. Regular doesn't have to mean frequent. You could adopt a slower, more punctuated approach and use a birthday or an annual review as a trigger for a conversation you revisit once a year.

A sense of an ending

Many of the podcast conversations I listen to vary wildly in time length. This isn't poor discipline on the part of the host, it shows that they are paying attention to whether the conversation is alive and that they are willing to close it down when it falters, whether that is after one hour or three. This is a contrast to meetings, which always take the time allotted to them, or traditional media like TV or radio, where time slots have to be filled. When you host conversations think podcast not broadcast. Try to feel when the conversation is done. Be willing to end early. Then, on the occasions when you run long, people will be more understanding.

Rather than grasping for a conclusion, notice when you become restless. Physical feelings are a great cue. Pay more attention to how the conversation feels than what the clock says. The ancient Greeks had two different words (and gods) for this — Chronos (or clock time) and Kairos (or felt time). Listen to Kairos. End when you feel you are done. Or, like the advice to stop eating before you are full, maybe even a little sooner. And to continue the culinary metaphor, remember to allow time after a conversation for digestion…

Feeding conversation

After space and time the third thing to think about is the material that you feed into the conversation. Even everyday office materials hold different possibilities. Whiteboard or flip chart? You can write things on both, but they feel different. The seed for this book was sown in an exploratory conversation captured on four huge whiteboards. If we'd only had a flip chart, I doubt I would have realised how rich the subject was.

Even different kinds of Post-its spawn different kinds of conversation. The giant, flip-chart-sized ones enable the conversation to cover a lot of territory. Tiny ones force you to work with one thought at a time. The ideas that became Yellow were born on groupings of A5-sized Post-its (you can guess which colour they were). If you have an aversion to Post-its, how about Artefact Cards? They are the size of playing cards, coloured on one side and white on the other. The fact they *aren't* sticky invites you to shuffle them around.

A cosmetics company I worked with had nearly two hundred products. One day we gathered every single bottle or tube in the room. This generated a powerful conversation about why there were so many, what they were, whether they were all needed and how they were best grouped. The physical presence of the products created a completely different conversation than we had had about exactly the same issues in umpteen previous meetings.

Participants come to leadership programmes in Oxford from all over the world. We ask them to bring an object from their own culture that has a personal story. We use this to start a conversation about who they are beyond their job title. With so many cultures in play, it is a colourful exercise, but you can do this with anyone — we all have different personal and familial cultures, even if we are from the same country.

You can also use an object to manage the rhythm of a conversation. For example, there is an ancient method, which has evolved in many cultures around the world, of using a talking stick (or stone) to govern who is able to speak. Only the person holding it can talk, the others must listen until the speaker puts the object down (we will consider a modern version, known as 'Unhurried Conversations', in more detail in Chapter 6). You might use a stick or a stone but you could also use a stapler or a sugar bowl. Which you choose will change how the conversation feels.

There are purpose-built materials you can use to act as prompts. Comedian Richard Herring has a book (and a website) of provocative 'Emergency Questions'. Diego Agulló, a Spanish artist and writer based in Berlin, has also co-authored a book of questions but with a more philosophical flavour. It is tiny, so you can carry it anywhere. The School of Life offers a box of cards with hundreds of different start points for conversation.

These props introduce an element of randomness and participation, relieving you of some responsibility (see Resources for links and Chapter 7 for notes on ways to use them).

Checklists are another kind of material you can use to catalyse a conversation. These often work by sleight of hand. It may seem that the Business Model Canvas, World Health Organization Surgical Checklist, or the creative brief in an advertising agency are an end in themselves but their real value lies in the conversations they provoke. In each case, a series of simple but searching questions force people into conversation about the business, patient or campaign. What goes on the piece of paper at the end is a useful reminder or point of reference, but it is the conversation that really matters. In Zen Buddhism, the stories or anecdotes masters use work in a similar way. They aren't tales with a simple moral, their value is in the conversations they provoke.

For the reading weekend that I host each year, the main material we use is the books, but we ask the participants to choose them. This means they are involved and have to take some responsibility before they even arrive, modelling the behaviour we want in the conversations. I say the main material because, as a residential event, the other important ingredient of the conversation is food.

Food and drink

Food and drink can refresh the conversation as well as the people. 'Let's have a coffee,' provides a pretext, duration, setting and mood in a single, well-understood phrase. When Nick asked me 'tea or whisky?' this was more than a choice of beverage — it was a choice about the kind of conversation I was up for (whisky would have suggested we were in for a late night).

What kind of food you offer is a prompt. If you want people to meet and mix, serve them food they have to pass around and share. Food also sends messages. When you accept another cup of tea or glass of wine, it is a signal you are willing to go on. If you decline the drink, you might also be declining more conversation, so if you can't bear to drink any more but want to keep talking, find a way to let your host know (you could always accept the drink and not drink it). If you are hosting and want to bring the conversation to a close, be wary of offering more refreshment.

How you show up

How you show up is about your energy, movement, position, posture, pace, gesture, tone, mood, use of language and so on. Not much then. It sends myriad signals about what is expected, what the norms are, what is regarded as important and so on. And all that happens in a matter of seconds.

Don't just assume that 'you are what you are' and you can't do anything about it. We all play different characters and roles. In Spanish there are two verbs 'to be' — one is used for those things that don't change — like where you are from (*soy ingles*). The other is used for things that vary — like being excited (*estoy animado*). This is the sense in which you can change how you show up.

If you show up in exactly the same way as you always do then people will understand that they are expected to act like they always do. And, 'If you do what you did, you're gonna get what you got.'[2] Which may be fine on occasions, but do you really want to have the same conversation over and over again?

First, notice what kind of inner state you are in. Are you calm, excited, bored, worried or curious? Ask yourself if that fits the kind of conversation you want to have. If it does, great, give yourself licence to show what you are feeling and express it physically, even if you don't talk about it.

If what you are feeling doesn't fit the conversation you want to have, consider whether now is the time to have it. If you have to go ahead anyway, acknowledge your inner state and take a few moments to consider how you could change it, even a little. If you are sleepy could you go outside for a minute before you start? If you are worried, imagine

---

2   I am sure many people have said this, but I first heard it in a gospel service at the Glide Memorial Church in San Francisco from the Reverend Ron Swisher. Amen.

a good outcome and feel into that, or just take a few deep, conscious breaths to reset your system. But don't just ignore how you are feeling and soldier on, going through the motions thoughtlessly.

If you can't embody an appropriate energy it won't matter what you say. The meta-messages that linguist and author Deborah Tannen talks of trump all that, just as 'culture eats strategy for lunch'. How you show up matters. If you are aware of that you can either change it or ask yourself if there is a way to use it (thereby 'using everything').

Clearing

There is art and craft in how you hold a conversation. Much of this work is clearing and setting. I think these words are great metaphors. A clearing in a forest is an open but bounded space, with distinct edges. A set in a theatre uses scenery and props to hold and shape the unfolding action. The discipline is to create defined and stimulating spaces and let action and words flow through them. Conversations are unpredictable, but here is something you can sensibly plan in advance. Let your controlling energy dwell on the materials and space rather than the people who inhabit it. The conversation will be all the better for it, though don't expect to get much credit; the better you do it the more invisible it becomes.

6
**Everything
changes,
everything
stays the same**

Nowadays, it is common to lament the decline or even death of conversation, particularly amongst young people, who (it is suggested) are either unwilling or unable to talk to someone else face to face. There are countless articles, books and talks bemoaning the effect of technology on how we talk to each other (or don't).

The technology may be new but the concern isn't. Writers and philosophers have been worried about it all the way back to Plato. The idea that conversation is becoming ever more superficial, corrupt and vulgar has been widespread for more than 2,000 years. What should we make of this?

I think the concern about conversation is a healthy sign and always has been. Whilst every generation likes to complain that 'things aren't what they were', there is more to it than this. There is no doubt that how we converse is changing and some of those changes look ugly, but if conversation didn't matter to us, we wouldn't make such a fuss. The fact that we are sensitive to it shows that we care and are paying attention. Long may that continue.

But it isn't constructive (or accurate) to catastrophise. Like people throughout history, we have little idea what will unfold from the challenges we face and it can be easier to reach a conclusion (however grim) than accept we don't know. The reality of our conversational lives is far more complex, uncertain and interesting than that. We are more resilient and creative than we give ourselves credit for.

So we should be concerned, but we shouldn't *only* be concerned. Above all we should humbly accept how little we can predict. All we can really be sure of is that conversation will change and people in the future will complain that it isn't what it used to be.

In an age of polarisation, it can feel like there are only two possibilities. The future is either like the Pixar film *Wall-E*, where we are wedded to our screens, unwilling (or unable) to utter a word to the person next to us, or it is a glorious, global meta-verse where anyone on the planet can talk to anyone else whenever they like. Neither of these is inevitable (or even likely). Technology is neither the death of conversation nor its saviour.

Resisting this neat dichotomy is a good in itself. Simply doing that already creates new possibilities. It opens a space to explore other perspectives and interpretations. It gives us the chance to learn and grow. It encourages nuance. It also comes quite naturally. Throughout history, our response to the changes brought about by technology, be it the invention of writing or the internet, has been vibrant and creative.

This is worth noticing. There is plenty to be curious about and take heart from. Our hold on conversation is not as fragile as we fear. The desire to be together in this particular way runs deep, so we use whatever is at hand to achieve it. We adapt, bend, hack, break, twist, combine and recombine whatever we are given to explore what is possible. This doesn't change.

The 'ceaseless, bubbling brew' of conversations we are part of generates a profusion of new ways to communicate all the time. Some of these emerge accidentally, others are the result of concerted effort. Some are serious, some are silly. Some go nowhere, others spread fast and, of those, some die off just as quickly whereas others become so normal we wonder how we ever did without them. Sometimes technology affords us genuinely novel opportunities, sometimes we find new ways to do old things and every now and then we resuscitate ancient forms of communication that it turns out we miss. What we don't do is nothing.

Writing ourselves off

Plato was worried about a new technology too — in his case, writing. He felt that unlike the ebb and flow of dialogue, written text would hinder true understanding and prevent ideas from being explored, questioned and refined, because it was fixed and static.

He had a point. Writing doesn't argue back. I once hurled a book across a room because it kept parroting the same things back to me, over and over again. Writing has enabled us to capture, keep, build and spread prodigious amounts of knowledge, but it has also introduced massive change and has some negative (side) effects. Few people alive today have the power of memory that our forebears did. Books can assume a weight beyond their worth. Filter bubbles and echo chambers are part of its legacy too because, like road rage, they are only possible at a distance. That remoteness — both physical and emotional — is only possible with the written word.

All in all, was the invention of writing a good thing? Who knows? Having started, it was never going to go away, even if it came at a cost. Not only have we found a million and one marvellous uses for it (like preserving what Plato said) but it has become part of who we are. Without the possibility of sacred texts, scientific theories or Shakespeare, the world as we know it simply wouldn't exist.

Another upheaval is going on now. In the period I have been working on this book Chat GPT has appeared, which has given me the chance to observe a disruptive novelty at first hand. What immediately struck me was the conversational name: *Chat* GPT. According to Chat GPT itself (bless), this choice reflected 'the model's capability to engage in back-and-forth interactions and produce text that feels like it could come from a human participant in a conversation'.

The focus on 'back-and-forth interactions' is so natural to human beings, that we design a machine to mesh with that and meet us where we are (though whether you feel it acts like a human or not is a bigger conversation).

In the space of about nine months, I have gone from astonishment to integration. I routinely consult it. I have my own sense of how it can help me and what to be wary of. I treat its responses a bit like those of an insanely well-read child. However, I do not, even for a second, mistake it for one. I am highly aware that this is just an appearance and that it is a completely different kind of entity from any organic being, well-read or otherwise.

Though the name tries to suggest otherwise, for me there is no sense in which my exchanges with it are conversation. For that, it would need to have an experience of its own, that can generate a field of conversation between us and allow two inner worlds to touch. It is incredibly impressive but that has only emphasised how much *more* impressive even ordinary human conversation is.

In my lifetime it is hard to recall a subject which has been talked about so intensely by so many people. For six months or so, it felt like no one talked about anything else, even in rural Spain. Open AI's Sam Altman echoed that in a response to a question about the ethics of the model. He said: 'We are in uncharted waters here. *Talking to smart people* is how we figure out what to do better.' Thus an immediate impact of a new technological form of 'chat' has been to stimulate a vast, dynamic, rich, ongoing and sometimes heated conversation amongst people.

Reaching back

Even as we reach forward to new technologies and innovations, we also reach back. In the 1990s physicist David Bohm responded to what he perceived as the fragmentation of thought and breakdown of communication in modern society by proposing the idea of 'Dialogue Circles'. These drew on ancient ideas expressed in Indian philosophy as well as the customs of indigenous tribes in North America.

Dialogue circles were designed to generate open and free-flowing conversations and enable groups of people to think and inquire together. These ideas and practices have spread widely and had a lasting effect. Bohm's work influenced Juanita Brown, who set up the World Cafe, another methodology for hosting conversation amongst groups. As a result of meeting Brown, Sarita Chawla set up a women's dialogue circle. Twenty-seven years later, it is still going.

Initiatives like this show up all over the place. Fed up with superficial conversation at networking events and frustrated by moving 'at the speed of the most impatient person in the room', facilitator Johnnie Moore developed a contemporary version of another ancient form of conversation. He calls them 'Unhurried Conversations' and they draw on the idea of using a talking object — traditionally a stick or a stone. The person speaking holds the object and cannot be interrupted until they have finished. Johnnie uses a sugar bowl or something else close to hand, but the talking object, whatever it is, guarantees that people are free to finish their thought (or not, as they wish). There are no introductions and the invitation is simply to share 'whatever is on your mind'. This invites pause and silence, as well as tangents and leaps. Though no theme is suggested, patterns often emerge.

Johnnie started to hold these conversations in cafes, open to anyone who wanted to join, and over the past few years he has done hundreds of them, in person and online. People keep coming back not just for the conversations but for the capacity they build. As one participant put it: 'Unhurried conversations train me to shut up and listen.' Such a simple structure is an easy way to create a different quality of conversation and people around the world have started leading their own.

The desire for conversation runs deep and, like a spring, we can't always divine where it will surface. There are many other initiatives which are implicitly, not explicitly, about conversation. The DO Lectures aren't only about the lectures, they are also about the conversation they generate over the course of the whole weekend. Likewise, book clubs aren't only about the books. Festivals create all kinds of containers for conversation. In the small town in Spain I call home there isn't one film club but two. One watches a film together then has a conversation about it. The other asks people to watch the film before they come, so the entire evening can be devoted to conversation.

Humans mess with everything

Whatever it is designed to do, technology elicits idiosyncratic responses from all of us. We are all constantly mucking about with how we use it — it is a highly creative arena. This shows up even in something as simple and basic as WhatsApp.

Throughout the writing of this book, I have been in a branching, rambling conversation with Nick Parker spread over many months and locations. As well as phone and video calls we have talked in Nick's shed, in the pub and in a muddy field at a festival in the rain.[1] Yet it was in the WhatsApp thread that he came up with the subtitle to this book. That thread wasn't separate from the rest of the conversation, it was woven into it. An increasingly rapid WhatsApp exchange would lead to a voice call, or a voice call would leave a trail of WhatsApp messages in its wake, making it hard to tell where the edges between one kind of conversation and another were, or if there were any.

Young people naturally mess around with technology and discover new possibilities inherent in it. This generates all sorts of behaviour — good, bad and ugly — but the idea that they are helpless sheep doesn't ring true to me. New generations always act in ways their elders don't understand or appreciate. One 20-something I met explained the capacity of WhatsApp to meet an ageless need — coping with the pain of heartbreak. He and a friend in a similar fix would 'converse' via voice messages 8–10 minutes long. This allowed them to craft what they said and raise things which could be difficult to say face to face. In the past they might have written letters but the technology

---

1   Nick crops up a few times in these pages because he is the friend with whom I have had the most conversations about conversation itself.

adds a new dimension. Voice messages drip with the additional meaning that comes with sound—rhythm, tone and inflection. Such 'thick' descriptions (as they are sometimes called) make it easier to communicate delicate emotions without needing to be a poet.

WhatsApp also affords entirely new possibilities. I can have a three-way conversation with the two of my sons who follow football without bothering the rest of the family, even when one of them is backpacking in Cambodia. This is so normal it is easy to forget how novel (and amazing) it is. I belong to another WhatsApp group where I have been playing an improv game called 'Djever' with four other people for nearly five years.[2] All we do is play the game (a version of 'word-at-a-time-story'). I asked the others what they get from it and their responses blew me away. They talked of joy, delight, acceptance and an 'uncomplicated and unconditional feeling of belonging' that comes from playing 'with other sentient beings that I carry around with me in my pocket'. Who would have imagined that could even be a thing? We do more with technology than anyone, even its designers, could have imagined or anticipated.

It's conversation (Jim), but not as we know it

But is this really conversation? Once again, what does it matter? These new forms may not be conversation as we know it, they may not have the same bandwidth or intensity as face-to-face conversation, but can we really be sure that they are not conversation at all? Just as speaking

---

2   Since Thursday, 25 October 2018, to be precise.

in person doesn't guarantee a conversation that brings you alive, a conversation via technology need not be deathly. It is not that simple.

Even as technology puts pressure on conversation 'as we know it' in one arena, it creates a whole new ecology of conversation somewhere else. There is a vast field of long, intimate, largely unedited conversations between individuals that now reach an audience of millions: podcasts. My experience, as a listener and as a guest, is that the more they feel like a proper conversation, the better they are. With Michael Garfield, on the 'Future Fossils' podcast (see Resources), I became so absorbed in the conversation that I forgot we were recording and found myself saying things I had never even thought before. This is completely different from a conventional media interview.

The concern about technology also risks idealising the past. Was there ever a golden age of conversation? In Plato's Athens, women had precious few opportunities to engage in dialogue and a significant proportion of the population were slaves. For much of the last few centuries, people laboured long hours in homes, factories or farms doing physically demanding and dangerous work, six or seven days a week. Was this really a garden of conversational delights?

Conventional, live conversation also has shortcomings we can be blind to. For example, most of the leadership courses and programmes I am involved with are short-lived. They don't allow for long, extended, slow-moving, iterated conversations. For many years I ignored that, even though I knew it was an Achilles heel. It took a pandemic to make me realise that technology can make up for this. Lengthy, regular conversations that play out over months, with people from all over the world, became not just possible but easy. You may lose bandwidth but you gain duration.

The technology also allowed us to explore new possibilities that face-to-face conversations lack. We could use art, music, film or poetry spontaneously, through live access to the wonders of the web. People being in different kinds of places can also be enriching. Technology enables a continuity and a kind of conversational field that simply isn't available in a workshop or on a short course at Oxford.

The critical faculty is alive and well

Critical responses to the state of conversation are often highly creative. People all over the world, with different interests and perspectives, are constantly experimenting with new formats that compensate for what they see as shortcomings and failings in the way we talk. Theodore Zeldin set up the Oxford Muse, with its menus of conversation, for exactly this purpose. The think tank Perspectiva is developing a slower, richer, more emotional form of conversation it calls the 'Antidebate' as a counterpoint to the polarising and corrosive effect of conventional argument.

In the political arena citizens' assemblies are becoming more prominent. They bring together people from across society to tackle complex and divisive issues — such as same-sex marriage and abortion (in Ireland). Participants feel a sense of responsibility and the nuanced, lengthy, deep conversations produce not just recommendations but a sense of empowerment and empathy. In short, people feel heard.

The Truth and Reconciliation Commission of post-apartheid South Africa was a radical and ground-breaking initiative, providing spaces where the testimony of perpetrators and victims of the violence could be heard.

When I visited South Africa in the midst of a state of emergency in 1985 no one imagined, even in their wildest dreams, that it would be possible to do something like that, but it was. This created a profound shift in our understanding of the role conversation could play in response to a traumatic past.

A lot happens out of sight. In the mid-1990s, I met a woman whose job was to convene conversations with people on opposite sides of a violent conflict. At the time she was working in Chechnya and Georgia. She would bring together groups of people who shared a professional interest — doctors or farmers, for instance — and talk with them about medicine or agriculture. Over time, the group would inch towards talking about the issues that divided them as well. She told me that whenever a new peace initiative is announced, it means people like her have been working behind the scenes, invisibly, often for years. Just because we don't see it, doesn't mean it isn't happening.

New kinds of conversation may also emerge obliquely, in places we don't expect. The European Organization for Nuclear Research (CERN) is an undertaking of extraordinary complexity and reach. It brings together thousands of scientists from all over the world to try and understand the fundamental structure of the universe. Arguably it is a massive conversation about what the world is made of. Along the way, and almost by accident, it gave birth to the World Wide Web (and many other innovations in fields as diverse as nuclear safety and medical imaging).

CERN is a living example of how to have highly complex conversations about huge questions with people from just about every place on the planet. Maybe it will also be the cradle of new understanding about how to host global conversations on issues other than physics? I am sure we could learn more about how to talk to each other as a global community from the scientists and technicians at CERN than we ever could from the politicians and diplomats at the UN.

It was complexity thinker Michael Dila who brought CERN to my attention. I was talking to him because of his work on what he calls 'System 3'.[3] This is another new initiative that hinges on conversation. Michael shares my belief that thinking goes on between us as well as within us. It is not only, or even primarily, an individual capacity. We cannot tackle, or even think well about, the 'wicked' problems we face alone. Conversation, he suggests, 'gives humans a mechanism for thinking together'. The immersive, connective, playful and improvisational nature of conversation generates a kaleidoscopic kind of thinking that is collective and connective. As a workshop participant said recently: 'Every time anyone says something my thinking shifts.' System 3 is a way of thinking about and designing such conversations.

These initiatives are just a few I have come across and are only a tiny fraction of what is going on. Their number, range and scope show how alive we are to the concerns regarding conversation and how creative we can be in response. That doesn't mean there will be no losses but, as with the invention of writing, there will also be 'invisible' gains we can't yet imagine. We should recognise and remember that we are both critical and creative.

3 The name refers so the two modes of thought famously described by Daniel Kahneman in *Thinking, Fast and Slow* (System 1 and System 2), which are both a feature of individual minds.

Life wants to connect

The wealth and diversity of these responses reflects something deep in our nature and in nature more generally. Life is precarious — finding something to eat whilst not being eaten is a struggle. One way living things respond to the challenge is to connect to each other. Over time, single-celled organisms come together to form multicellular ones. Connections proliferate; highly interwoven systems of cells and organs co-evolve and eventually lead to complex beings like oysters, octopuses or ourselves. Even trees which stand apart in a forest are connected under the ground, via their roots, sharing both nutrients and information. Whales within a given population also sing common songs, with slight variations that evolve over time. The entire population may share a similar 'theme' but individual whales contribute their own version of the theme.

Within our own bodies, immune cells and neurones share a lot of signalling molecules, so they can 'talk' to each other. Scientists have learned to follow, developing ways to talk to each other across different disciplines such as oncology and immunology, in order to understand the conversation that is going on within our own bodies. One of the stories of life is the story of ever-increasing connection and complexity.

Alone, we are no one. Like other living things, we long for the joy, delight and solace that connection with others brings. Relationships are vital to us and conversation is one of the most important ways we have of forming, cultivating and deepening those relationships. Part of the everyday miracle of conversation is that the sense of me being separate from you can dissolve, if not disappear altogether.

Conversation is difficult. And we can't do without it. Which is why we show such concern about it and find so many ways to create and re-create it. Rather than leaping to a conclusion of triumph or disaster it seems to me that it is both wiser and more effective to accept, hold and enjoy the paradox.

7
**Maxims
and mantras**

The conversational world is awash with beguiling lists of 'tips and tricks' that promise to improve your conversation. After a year or so spent talking, reading, thinking and writing about conversation, I thought I would compile my own. What are the reminders or nudges that feel most important and practical to me? What do I want to emphasise or ignore, juxtapose or combine? What advice would I give myself?

My list has a different flavour from most. The kind of ideas I have picked out make (broad) suggestions about what to do, but they also reflect an attitude, almost a philosophy of conversation. To reflect this I have called them 'maxims and mantras'. A maxim is 'a short phrase that expresses a general truth'. A mantra is a word or sound repeated to aid concentration (and though it comes from meditation it is also used in improvisational theatre).

I don't intend my list to be comprehensive, exclusive or definitive. It is not a linear process of steps to go through in order, nor is there any magic (or science) to the fact there are twenty. There is variety within it. It will change over time but here is what I have now:

1. Have conversations. Don't avoid them.

2. Do not treat a conversation as a competition.

3. Converse like yourself. No one else can.

4. It isn't all about you — conversation is a co-creation.

5. Pay attention to how you pay attention.

6. Don't just ask questions; don't just make statements.

7. Talk to people who aren't like you.

8. Be interested not interesting.

9. Listen with your body and to your body.

10. Be open to tangents and digressions
   (good stuff can come from the edge).

11. If there is no silence, there is no conversation.

12. If you are stuck or tense, breathe.

13. Be willing to be interrupted.

14. Do not be vehement. At least, not all the time.

15. Be playful.

16. Notice more, let go, use everything.

17. Make lots of offers, see lots of offers.

18. Remember you have a body. Use it.

19. Be willing to stay in uncertainty and doubt.

20. Don't rely on lists, even this one.

There are many ways you can use these ideas. The maxims and mantras are connected but offer different ways in. It reminds me of when I used to skateboard. Sometimes I found it helpful to think about the position of my head. On other days that didn't work, so instead I would focus on flexing my knees, or the angle of my hips. Having a variety of places to start helps.

Some of them are physical actions (e.g. breathe), others capture an attitude (e.g. be playful), but they are all touchstones to return to repeatedly. They encourage reflection as well as action. For example, 'Talk to people who aren't like you' invites me to consider what I am 'like'. 'Be willing to be interrupted' might get me thinking about why I am attached to my own ideas.

I don't need to make them visible in order to be valuable: I might just hold one in mind. If I drift off or get lost, they give me somewhere to come back to. Nor do I have to do all of them. I might use one in conversation with my sons and another one with a colleague.

I could try building on strength or correcting for weakness (which would make me think about my conversational strengths and weaknesses). If I get stuck or bored with one of them, I can let it go and try something else.

I could pick a single mantra and work with that. As NPR (National Public Radio) journalist Celeste Headlee says in her TED talk: 'Choose one and master it and you will already enjoy better conversations.'[1]

Each of them could lead to many different actions. For example, 'Remember you have a body; use it', might remind me to lean into a conversation, literally and metaphorically. On a different day the same mantra might

---

1   She said this of her own 'Ten Basic Rules for Better Conversation' but it works equally well for these maxims and mantras.

suggest a walk and talk. Or it might help me notice my own restlessness and bring a conversation to an end.

Hold things lightly

It should be clear by now that what we like about lists — that they are short, simple and clear — is also a weakness. When we reduce things in the way I just have, something important is left out.

Remember this. The desire for simplicity and clarity needs to be tempered with a recognition that life is not actually like that. Statistician George Box captured this beautifully when he said, 'All models are wrong; and some of them are useful.' This is why I included the last mantra ('Don't rely on lists') — it reminds me to hold the others lightly.

In conversation, there are always creative tensions in play that pull in different directions — for example, speaking versus listening, relevance versus digression, colour versus advance. What to do at any particular moment is a moving target. The shifting, fluid and unpredictable nature of conversation is the source of both the difficulty and the delight of it.

My list suits me but you are different from me. You have to think for yourself. There may be maxims or mantras here that you can use immediately; there might be others you can't, or don't want to, or don't need. Some of it might make sense now, some might not make sense until later, possibly quite a long time later.

To borrow from the writer Simon Sarris: 'If [the suggestions] are forceful, it is simply because they are mine. Take what you wish.' Use my list to make your own. Bend, twist or combine my maxims and mantras to suit yourself.

Borrow from other lists. Drop what you don't need or doesn't work for you. Don't expect you will ever be 'done'. What you want is to be able to generate a sensitive series of timely responses to the challenges you are interested in — much like a conversation itself. Make your practice of conversation an ongoing conversation with yourself.

Ready-made help

There is plenty of help out there you can easily get your hands on. You can buy packs of cards or books, full of questions and conversation starters (see Resources). This gives you some freedom because it is clear the questions aren't yours, but you still have to think about how to use them.

For example, Tim Yearsley's experience with young adults is that prompt cards work best as 'an enabling constraint'. Give people too many and they just rifle through them, responding instantly or skipping over ones they don't like. That doesn't generate conversation.

Think about whether you let people choose their own cards or deal them at random. Do you select single cards, a small set or the whole deck? Does everyone answer the same question or not? Who goes first? How long do you stick with each question? What follow-up questions might you use? As you can see, using prepared questions generates yet more questions.

Not everything has to be a question either. Conversations can start with an observation, a statement, a gesture, a sound or a look. Understanding this (see #6 above) takes the pressure off thinking of a 'great' question and creates more variety. A great question to ask now might not be tomorrow, or with a different person, so loosening your attachment to questions can make you more sensitive to context.

Do it yourself

As with the maxims and mantras, I encourage you to come up with your own prompts. Theodore Zeldin did that with his 'conversation menus'. If you look at the 'conversation starter' material that is out there you can see that it falls into distinct categories, like these:

— **Dichotomies** (e.g. 'in or out?'; 'city or country?'): *Forced choices, often between ambiguous alternatives, that invite people to think about what matters most to them.*

— **Heart's desire/no limits** (e.g. 'a quality you lack, that you wish you had?'; 'if you could solve one global problem, what would it be?'): *Stripping away practical limits and norms invites someone to consider what it is they care about.*

— **Reflection on self and past** (e.g. 'something you regret?'): *Self-examination, whether moral or practical, reveals character and gets people thinking about how things could have been otherwise.*

— **Different perspective in time** (e.g. 'what would you tell your 10-year-old self?'): *Shifting in time — normally to the end of life or childhood — is a way of getting an outside perspective on yourself and what matters.*

— **Metaphor** (e.g. 'what animal do you see yourself as?'): *Use metaphor to open up a different way to see something, or yourself.*

— **A specific experience** (e.g. 'least favourite haircut?'): *Ordinary details, when put in the spotlight, open things up or make them visible.*

This gives you another option. Instead of buying a set of someone else's questions, use these categories to generate your own. Sitting down with colleagues or friends to do so could be a powerful conversation in itself.

You will notice that all of these are different ways to break a routine and invite someone, obliquely, to reveal a little more of themselves and their view of the world, without asking intrusive questions. This is a riff on one of the tools I introduced in Chapter 4. (Maybe I should add 'Pay attention to conversational routines' to the list of mantras…?)

You see, my own list is changing already. Allow that to happen. Use whatever tips, tools and models you find useful but think of them as scaffolding, that you can change as you see fit, to support what you want to make. This means developing what the poet John Keats called 'negative capability'. This is the capacity 'of being in uncertainties, mysteries, doubts, without any irritable reaching after fact and reason'. If you want to fixate on something, make it the ability to stay open (see #19 above).

Only snake-oil salesmen promise 'secrets' that enable you to have 'deep' or 'meaningful' conversations 'in any and every situation, with anyone' and appear 'instantly interesting'. Forget that. To rework what Shunryu Suzuki said to his students: 'You are perfect as you are; and you could use a little improvement.' How about that as a mantra?

The dance of conversation

Conversation is oxymoronic. It is bittersweet. We have extraordinary skill yet feel incompetent. We crave connection but are nervous of each other. We yearn to be seen as long as we are also free to hide. We want surprises we can control. We feel conversation is in decline even as we create new ways to do it.

These are not contradictions to be resolved but paradoxes to be held. It is the tension between opposing poles that gives rise to conversation as a dynamic, creative force. To live and breathe is to ebb and flow, and conversation is a living thing. The challenge is not to reach (or even seek) a fixed point but to sense and feel (as well as decide or choose) in which direction it is fitting to move next.

Conversation is a musical thing, like jazz or birdsong: more 'call and response' than question and answer. It enables us to travel great distances, but the joy is in the journey not the destination. We are meant to sing and dance along the way, jamming with others, riffing off them, creating something new right here, right now, in a way that no one can alone.

Each of us has the chance to cultivate a local space of pattern, sense and meaning — an oasis, where we can think and be together. This is an end in itself. It can also be a crucible, where we develop responses to meet the complex predicaments and crises that we face — personal, social, political or ecological. Each of these domains can influence the others: local patterns influence global patterns, as well as vice versa.

Your own sensations and observations are the raw material, not some magical ingredient from elsewhere. Conversation thrives on variety and no one does it quite like you. The aim isn't to become good at conversation, it is to become good at being you, in conversation.

Later today you will have a conversation of some kind. When you do, you have the precious chance to connect with your own experience and the people you are talking with and, as a result, become more alive. Never cease to be amazed by this. However common it may be, it is also extraordinary — miraculous even. Through us, the universe is somehow able to talk to itself.

Conversation is a musical thing, like jazz or birdsong: more 'call and response' than question and answer. It enables us to travel great distances, but the joy is in the journey not the destination.

Resources

Books & Poetry
I read many books about conversation, but one that stands out (and stands the test of time) is *Conversation* by Theodore Zeldin.
In addition:
The Art of Gathering, Priya Parker (Penguin, 2019)
The Conversation Book, Diego Agulló & Dmitry Paranyushkin (Circadian, 2021)
Fierce Conversations, Susan Scott (Penguin, 2022)
On Dialogue, David Bohm (Routledge, 2004)
'*What you missed that day you were absent from fourth grade*', Brad Aaron Modlin, *onbeing.org/poetry*

Musings & Talks
Chimamanda Ngozi Adichie, 'The danger of a single story' *ted.com/talks*
Adam Mastroianni for floating, doorknobs and more *adammastroianni.com*
Michael Garfield, The Future Fossils Podcast
Theodore Zeldin, *oxfordmuse.com*

Prompts & Tools
Artefact Cards
smithery.com/artefact-cards
Emergency questions
rhlstprhlstp.com/emergency-questions-2
Conversation Starter Cards, The School of Life
theschooloflife.com
Unhurried Conversations
unhurried.org/conversations

About the author

Robert Poynton divides his time between an off-grid, solar-powered house near Arenas de San Pedro (in rural Spain) and Oxford, where he is an Associate Fellow of Green Templeton College and the Saïd Business School.

At Oxford his work is practical not academic — the workshops and programmes he runs are designed to help leaders have conversations they don't normally have. He has also worked with clients such as the BBC, Chanel, Merck, Unilever and Airbus.

In Spain he hosts experiential events for individuals like Reading Retreats — which use books to spark off conversation — or the Creative Tapas Experience, a rapid process of collaborative making which catalyses a wealth of creative conversations.

He is also the co-founder of Yellow learning (an online learning experience based on conversation) and On Your Feet (an improv-based consultancy). He has spoken and led workshops at the DO Lectures, the Skoll World Forum, the d-school at Stanford University, Singularity University and Schumacher College. He is the author of *Do Pause: You are not a To Do list* (Do Books, 2019) and *Do Improvise: Less push. More pause. Better results. A new approach to work (and life)* (Do Books, 2013, updated 2022).

He is married with three sons. His wife runs an organic beef farm.

@robpoynton | robertpoynton.com

Thanks

The idea for this book occurred in a conversation with Jim Marsden, so heartfelt thanks to him for that and for showing me that conversation is not the sole preserve of the talkative. Also, for the images that adorn it; it is lovely that he is part of the finished book as well.

The book also came into being through conversations with more people than it is possible to remember or recognise. If you have had a conversation with me in the last couple of years, then you have been part of its development, whether you realised it or not. Thanks to each and every one of you for your ideas and inspiration. Some of those I can name include Claus Jacobs, David Keating, Fateme Banishoeib, John Oliver, Julie Batty, Mark Barden, Stefan Cousquer, Steve Chapman and Tom Chatfield.

Those I haven't named include anyone and everyone who has been part of Yellow in any capacity over the past three years. Thanks to Neil Baker for first calling my attention to this when he said: 'If Yellow has a methodology, it is probably conversation.'

Thanks to Alex Carabi for all the conversations in both holding and designing Yellow. Thanks also for the initial conversation about the Stoics. Without that tangent, none of this would exist at all.

Thanks to Tim Yearsley for your enthusiasm and for the question, 'Is improv conversation or is conversation improv?' To Gary Hirsch for decades of improvisational conversation. To Justin Wise, for Hyde Park and Heidegger and the chance to have such long, flowing, unfettered conversation. To Sarita Chawla, for sharing your dedication to dialogue. To Roland Harwood for reassuring me I had something worth saying.

To TOGA (Jason Trew) for persisting through the practical difficulties when we first tried to speak and to Lucy Taylor for introducing us. To Leila Ferreira for contacting me about *Do Pause*, and for the opportunity to spend time in Cascais (again) when the heat at home was too much. That place is in this book.

To Tracey Camilleri, for ten years of design conversation and for showing me what it means to be 'collegiate'. To Marshall Young — a master of mealtime conversation. To the city and the University of Oxford where conversation is in the ether, and in particular to the Taylorian Library, where conversation is forbidden, enabling me to spend so many quiet hours writing about it.

To Jorge Alvarez, an Olympic conversationalist. Maybe one day, we will be able to answer Lea's question directly. To Johnnie Moore, who has an ability to notice and call out what is going on in real time in a conversation like no one I know — 'Unhurried' has been a gift that keeps on giving, to me and to the world. To Antony Quinn for your own role in that and for re-routing your trip to London that day — never has a stand-up conversation on a train been so useful. Thanks also for the introduction to Syrus Lowe, from whom I borrowed the idea of 'finding your full stop'.

To Alana Hockridge for showing me that age is no barrier to a great conversation. To Theo Kelly for the questions in the furniture van. To Alex Flemming, for the insights about how cells talk and scientists talk about them. To Neil Randhawa, whose first comment to me at the Do Lectures in 2011 catapulted us straight through the small talk into a lifelong friendship.

To Neena Sims, Lizzie Winn and the other members of 'Top First, Then Pants'. When you host so many conversations, it is great to have the chance to be in a quality conversation as 'just' a participant.

To Michael Dila, for articulating the ideas of System 3, for the conversations that has led to and for what is yet to come, whatever that may be.

To Aaron Deemer for the conversation that emerges from embodiment. Thanks also for the poem 'What You Missed That Day You Were Absent from Fourth Grade' (and thanks to Brad Aaron Modlin for writing it).

To my family across generations — to my parents and my sisters for creating the cradle of my conversational life. To my wife — conversation with you is both the crucible and the substance of our relationship. To my children Mateo, Pablo and Bruno — you may not realise it, but the chance to have a conversation with any of you, together or alone, whether it is about 'the important stuff' or not, is a mouth-watering prospect and one of the delights of my life.

A huge shout-out to Nick Parker. In the Singapore Botanic Gardens it felt like we were continuing a conversation from another life, not meeting for the first time. Thanks for the illustrations, ideas, links, suggestions, comments, support, critique, laughs and, above all, for being so available for conversation along the way. Your name really should be on the front of this book, I couldn't possibly have done it without you. Apart from the mistakes. Those I can manage on my own.

Finally, to Jess, Anya, Wilf and Miranda for working the Do Books magic. When we first spoke at the Do Lectures in 2011, I never imagined there would be not just one book but three, all of them connected, flowing out of and into each other. It really is quite amazing what a single conversation can lead to...

Books in the series

Also available

⊗DO⊗
Book Co

Available in print, digital and audio formats from booksellers or via our website: **thedobook.co**. To hear about events and forthcoming titles, find us on social media **@dobookco**, or subscribe to our newsletter.